Writers and Age

ALSO BY ESTHER HARRIOTT

*American Voices: Five Contemporary Playwrights
in Essays and Interviews*
(McFarland, 1988; paperback 2013)

Writers and Age

Essays on and Interviews with Five Authors

Esther Harriott

McFarland & Company, Inc., Publishers
Jefferson, North Carolina

"For the Word Is Flesh." "Postscript." Copyright 1930, © 1955 by Stanley Kunitz, from *The Poems of Stanley Kunitz 1928–1978* by Stanley Kunitz. Used by permission of W. W. Norton & Company, Inc.

"As Flowers Were." Copyright © 1958, © 1979 by Stanley Kunitz, "Father and Son." Copyright 1944, © 1971 by Stanley Kunitz, "The Portrait." Copyright © 1971 by Stanley Kunitz, "After The Last Dynasty." Copyright © 1962 by Stanley Kunitz, "Three Floors," "King of the River." Copyright © 1971 by Stanley Kunitz, "Indian Summer at Land's End," "The Knot." Copyright © 1979 by Stanley Kunitz, "Quinnapoxet," "Route Six," "The Layers." Copyright © 1978 by Stanley Kunitz, "The Snakes of September." "The Round." "Passing Through." Copyright © 1985 by Stanley Kunitz, "Halley's Comet." "Touch Me." Copyright © 1995 by Stanley Kunitz, "The Long Boat." Copyright © 1985 by Stanley Kunitz, from *The Collected Poems* by Stanley Kunitz. Used by permission of W. W. Norton & Company, Inc.

LIBRARY OF CONGRESS CATALOGUING-IN-PUBLICATION DATA

Harriott, Esther.
    Writers and age : essays on and interviews with five authors / Esther Harriott.
       p.   cm.
    Includes bibliographical references and index.

    ISBN 978-0-7864-3439-8 (softcover : acid free paper) ∞
    ISBN 978-1-4766-1796-1 (ebook)

    1. American literature—20th century—History and criticism. 2. Old age in literature. 3. Aging in literature. 4. Authors, American—20th century—Interviews. 5. Older people's writings, American—History and criticism.   I. Title.
PS228.O43H37 2015
810.9'354—dc23
                                                  2014037183

BRITISH LIBRARY CATALOGUING DATA ARE AVAILABLE

© 2015 Esther Harriott. All rights reserved

No part of this book may be reproduced or transmitted in any form or by any means, electronic or mechanical, including photocopying or recording, or by any information storage and retrieval system, without permission in writing from the publisher.

On the cover: *Man Writes a Letter*, 1910 © 2015 PicturesNow

Printed in the United States of America

McFarland & Company, Inc., Publishers
   Box 611, Jefferson, North Carolina 28640
      www.mcfarlandpub.com

For my son, Billy

Acknowledgments

Interviewing the five writers—V. S. Pritchett, Stanley Kunitz, Doris Lessing, Mavis Gallant, and Russell Baker—was one of my greatest pleasures in writing this book about them.

My thanks to Oliver Pritchett for giving me permission to publish my interview with his late father, V. S. Pritchett, and to Chuck Verrill, Stanley Kunitz's agent and friend, for permission to publish my interview with Kunitz, which originally appeared in slightly different form as "I'm Not Sleepy" in *Interviews and Encounters with Stanley Kunitz* (Riverdale-on-Hudson, NY: Sheep Meadow Press, 1993). My interview with Doris Lessing, copyright © 1992 Doris Lessing, is printed by kind permission of Jonathan Clowes Ltd., London, on behalf of Doris Lessing.

All excerpts from the poems of Stanley Kunitz are used by permission of W. W. Norton & Company, Inc., and I am grateful to Elizabeth Clementson, permissions manager, for her savvy and sensitivity.

Table of Contents

Acknowledgments   6
Introduction   9

1. V. S. Pritchett   19
2. Interview with V. S. Pritchett   45
3. Stanley Kunitz   52
4. Interview with Stanley Kunitz   65
5. Doris Lessing   74
6. Interview with Doris Lessing   96
7. Mavis Gallant   105
8. Interview with Mavis Gallant   134
9. Russell Baker   149
10. Interview with Russell Baker   178

Chapter Notes   189
Index   195

Introduction

> To get a glimpse of what it means to be old you have to leave science behind for a while and consult literature, not "the literature," as we call our compendiums of research, just plain old pure literature.—Lewis Thomas, M.D., *The Fragile Species*

"The inescapability of old age is now secretly the new predicament," Ronald Blythe observed in *The View in Winter*, his study of aging in the twentieth century, when average life expectancy almost doubled in the industrialized world. As the words "inescapability" and "predicament" suggest, Blythe's view of the phenomenon was ambivalent. People born in the twentieth century would live much longer than their ancestors in earlier centuries, but they also "faced the likelihood of a long old age."[1] Blythe pointed out that most of them "were not involved in the aging process and seemed to have lived without thought or preparation for it. It is one of the essential ways in which our forebears differed from us" (3).

Theirs was a world "where it was the exception to go grey, to reach the menopause, to retire, to become senile," and where "the knowledge of the destruction of the physical self was quite unlike anything we understand." This meant that, "for all their fatal illnesses, people were once vital, capable, and very much alive up to the edge of their graves" (3–4). "Perhaps," he concluded, "with full-span lives the norm, people may need to learn how to be aged as they once had to learn to be adult" (22).

But there are few models to learn from in life, where a full old age is something new, or in literature, whose principal themes—love, war, adventure, politics, crime, the coming-of-age—are embodied in the young protagonists. Old age has been a secondary theme and old men and women secondary characters. Shakespeare's *King Lear* and Sophocles' *Oedipus at Colonus* are the only great literary works whose heroes are old men; and Sophocles, who completed the play in his ninetieth year, the only great writer who depicted old age with first-hand knowledge of the subject.

Images of Age: Past

Unlike the many visual representations of age produced through the centuries by painters and sculptors in their seventies, eighties, and even nineties (so many that art historians coined the term *Altersstil*, old-age style), the literary representations of age were by writers younger than their aged characters (including Shakespeare), who drew on stereotypes of age that went back to ancient times. What their works shared—including the acknowledged masterpieces—was an emphasis on age's infirmities and indignities.

Chaucer was in his forties and fifties when he created his lascivious and impotent old men in *The Canterbury Tales*, whose lust for young women made them objects of ridicule. In "The Merchant's Tale," January, the rich old bachelor knight who marries young May, is still virile; but Chaucer shows the bride's disgust when she beholds her husband's worn and withered body on their wedding night. She soon finds a handsome young lover and the old husband assumes his inevitable role of the cuckold.

Shakespeare made Falstaff immortal in *Henry IV* as a comic old rogue and companion in mischief to the young Prince Hal; but when the Lord Chief Justice reprimands Falstaff for his destructive pranks, he also mocks him, in a tirade of negative images of age, for trying to appear young:

> Do you set down your name in the scroll of youth, that are written down old with all the characters of age? Have you not a moist eye, a dry hand, a yellow cheek, a white beard, a decreasing leg, and increasing belly? Is not your voice broken, your wind short, your chin double, your wit single, and every part of you blasted with antiquity? And will you yet call yourself young?[2]

In *Henry IV, Part II*, Prince Hal, now newly crowned King Henry V, responds to Falstaff's fond greeting with a curt and cold dismissal of his former companion and a rebuke to his inappropriately youthful behavior: "I know thee not old man.... How ill white hairs become a fool and jester!"[3]

Jonathan Swift was fifty-seven when he wrote the third book of *Gulliver's Travels* and its story of the Struldbrugs, who, granted eternal life without eternal youth, grow old and are unable to die. Here is Swift's cruel picture of the Struldbrugs in old age, with the usual afflictions of disease, dementia, and decrepitude unrelieved by death:

> They lose their teeth and hair, they have ... no distinction of taste, but eat and drink ... without relish or appetite. The diseases they were subject to still continue without increasing or diminishing. In talking, they forget the common appellation of things and the names of persons, even those who are their nearest friends and relations.[4]

Images of Age: Present

To cite examples closer to our own time, the twentieth-century writers who depicted old age, like their literary antecedents in the past, had not yet reached that stage of life themselves and emphasized its horrors. Samuel Beckett (at forty-seven) wrote his trilogy of novels, *Molloy*, *Malone Dies*, and *The Unnamable*, three portraits of old age as it moves from senility to the dying of the senses to total helplessness; and W. B. Yeats (at sixty) published *The Tower*, with its searing title poem in which he rails against "Decrepit age that has been tied to me / As to a dog's tail."[5]

A true picture of old age was just as elusive in twentieth-century American society, which inherited, and perpetuated, the negative myths of the past. The politically incorrect stereotypes of "little old ladies" and "old geezers" may have been replaced by the condescending euphemisms of "senior citizens" and "golden agers," but the images of old age—frail, feeble, sexless, senile—remained unchanged.

What *did* change were the demographics. In the last decade of the twentieth century, as advertisers recognized that the aging population—especially the aging and affluent boomers—offered a growing new market, they began to show "positive" images of age (silver-haired couples on

Introduction

romantic cruises, mountain-climbing grandfathers) on television and in popular magazines. But the message was the same: youth was the ideal. Aging well meant looking and acting young.

This message found its apotheosis in the proliferating new genre of "self-help" books for the aging (as though aging were a problem that could be fixed), which offered a vision of a "new old age" that was nothing like the old age of the past. In *New Passages: Mapping Your Life Across Time*, by Gail Sheehy (Random House, 1995), the archetype of the genre, the author reported the discovery of a new stage of life that she called "Second Adulthood." Because of longer life spans, she explained, the old demarcations of life's stages were out of date. Middle age now began at sixty and continued to the age of seventy-five; a fifty-year-old woman (which happened to be the age of the oldest members of the boomer generation) could look forward to celebrating her ninetieth birthday—provided she took care of herself (a core belief among boomers).

Successful Aging, by John W. Rowe, M.D., and Robert L. Kahn, M.D. (Pantheon, 1998), based on ten years of studies of men and women of seventy and older, was one of the first contributions to the genre by members of the medical profession. Noting that "people often blame aging for losses that are ... caused by life style," the doctors concluded from their findings that "old people who are physically fit are at lower risk of death than nonsmokers with normal blood pressure who are couch potatoes." Their overall conclusion: "You are responsible for your own old age."[6]

The review of their book in the *New York Times* was accompanied by pictures and descriptions of two people who were identified as examples of "successful aging":

> Malcolm Clarke, 93 ... plays an hour and a half to two hours of doubles tennis four times a week. He took up "serious tennis" at 75 and has since won 38 national championships, playing annually in a national tournament for those 85 and older.... Helen Page, 83 ... is a survivor ...[of] breast cancer ... [and] a couple of heart attacks. After a near-vegetarian diet ... and daily exercise (a two-mile walk before breakfast), a second angiogram showed she no longer needed bypass surgery.[7]

Perhaps the doctors intended to demolish the negative images of age as an inevitable decline into decrepitude, but if these were their

Introduction

examples of "successful aging," were they suggesting that the elderly who didn't play tennis, become vegetarians, walk two miles before breakfast, or the equivalents, were failures?

These prototypes have been followed by a steady flow of self-help books on aging by gurus with and without medical degrees. While their recommendations differ in the details, the implied result of following them is the same: you will not only live far longer than those who lived in previous generations, you will also be (to quote Gail Sheehy) "better, stronger, deeper, wiser, funnier, freer, sexier, and more attentive to living those privileged moments."[8]

But the so-called positive new myths of age merely stand the negative old myths on their heads, replacing the dread of age with denial. To prepare for this stage of life that for most of us will likely be a long one, we need a clear-eyed view of what it is really like. For that, in the words of the physician and writer Lewis Thomas, quoted in the epigraph to this introduction, we "have to … consult literature."

This book consults the literature of five great writers: V. S. Pritchett, Stanley Kunitz, Doris Lessing, Mavis Gallant, and Russell Baker. Born between 1900 (Pritchett) and 1925 (Baker), they belong to the first generation of the twentieth century and to the first generation of writers able to write about old age from experience. In their later works we can read about growing old, as reported by the old, not as imagined or observed by the young and middle-aged.

Voices of Experience

The writers acquired their common mother tongue in far-flung parts of the English-speaking world: Pritchett in England, Kunitz and Baker in the United States, Lessing in the former British colony of Southern Rhodesia (now Zimbabwe), and Gallant in Canada. Both Lessing and Gallant emigrated before launching their writing careers: Lessing moved to England in 1949, shortly before her thirtieth birthday, and Gallant to France in 1950, at the age of twenty-eight.

As members of a generation, they shared many formative experiences. All of them lived through the changes and upheavals of a turbulent century—the Great Depression, the Second World War (Pritchett, born in 1900, and Kunitz, born in 1906, also lived through the First World War), the Cold War years, the political and social rebellions of the 1960s and 1970s, the revolutions in science and technology—that transformed their societies and were reflected in their writing. And all of them were recognized for their work with the highest honors and awards bestowed in their respective countries.

As they aged themselves, the writers turned more to the subject of age in their writing, not as a unique or self-contained stage of life, but as a continuation—another context in which to pursue the themes of their earlier poems, novels, stories, and essays. And those who had written about love—a central theme of fiction and poetry—now wrote about love in old age, an unfamiliar theme and, for some readers, an embarrassing one.

V. S. Pritchett, England's preeminent man of letters for more than six decades of the twentieth century, wrote about the continuation of passionate love in old age in two late memoirs (at seventy and eighty) and two late review-essays of books about growing old. But his belief in the transforming power of love in old age was given its fullest expression in his late stories. The protagonists of Pritchett's two late love stories examined in this book are both seventy, both retired, both widowers; otherwise they are completely different in character and circumstances.

The protagonist of "The Spree," a retired commercial traveler, is one of Pritchett's comic characters, a blowhard given to lofty pronouncements and grandiose gestures; but we see the grief under his comic surface and his awkward, touching attempts to fill the emptiness left by his wife's death. The protagonist of "On the Edge of the Cliff," a retired botany professor, erudite and charming, lives happily with a beautiful young painter, who reciprocates his love. Yet he, too, feels the losses and vulnerabilities of old age and his awareness of his own mortality gives particular poignancy to his love affair.

Stanley Kunitz gave the lie to Wordsworth's famous dictum, "We Poets in our youth begin in gladness, / But thereof come in the end despondency and madness." Kunitz not only continued to write poems through his sixties, seventies, and eighties; he wrote his best poems in those decades. He kept the themes of his earlier poetry—sexual love, the search for his father, the natural world—but he removed the excesses and ornamentation of his early style, making his later poetry simpler and more powerful.

Many of Kunitz's late poems are erotic, not only his love poems to his wife, the last of which, "Touch Me," he wrote in his ninetieth year, but also his poems about the natural world—poems like "King of the River," in which he portrays the young salmon's swimming upstream to spawn as the youthful drive to sexual consummation, or "The Snakes of September," with its startling image of the pair of snakes that the poet sees in his garden, "dangling head-down, entwined / in a brazen love-knot."[9] The garden itself, where so many of Kunitz's poems are located, embodies the cycle of birth, death, and rebirth that is the overarching theme of all his poetry.

Doris Lessing wrote in many genres and on many themes, but she is known best for her realistic novels dissecting the lives of women at different ages and at different moments of the twentieth century. She addressed the political, social, moral, and intellectual issues that concerned her quasi-autobiographical protagonists and she dramatized her protagonists' personal lives, especially their troubled relationships with their lovers. These two broad themes are divided between two linked novels, *The Diary of a Good Neighbor* and *If the Old Could...*, published together in one volume as *The Diaries of Jane Somers*, Lessing's first novel about old age.

The first of these, *The Diary of a Good Neighbor*, is an unflinching study of a ninety-two-year-old woman living alone in a Council flat—the English equivalent of "the projects"—in late-twentieth-century London. Through the sharp observations of the old woman by her middle-aged neighbor, Jane Somers (the protagonist and Lessing's alter ego), the reader is made almost viscerally aware of how it feels to be old. Characteristically, Lessing-Jane also grapples with the political and moral questions raised by extended old age in a society ill-prepared to cope with it.

If the Old Could..., set five years later, continues Jane's investigations of old age; but the focus of this companion novel is on her awareness of her own aging and her fear of losing the sexual attractiveness that has been so important to her sense of identity. Lessing probed this subject

Introduction

more deeply twelve years later in her next novel, *Love, Again*, in which she examined the various forms of love (romantic, platonic, maternal, etc.); but the emotional center of the novel is the anguish of an aging woman as she confronts the end of her youth and her sexual life.

The underlying theme of Mavis Gallant's huge body of short stories is the effect of the Second World War on the lives of the people who lived through it. Grouped in decades, from the "Thirties and Forties" to the "Eighties and Nineties," according to when they take place, not when they were written, the stories are also painstakingly accurate records—historic, geographic, political—of their various locations. But, like all great fiction, Gallant's stories live in their characters. In her earlier stories they included Eastern Europeans who had left their countries and moved to Paris after the war. In these late stories—set late in the twentieth century and written late in Gallant's life—the émigrés have grown old and are facing death. Gallant writes movingly about the depth of love between the long-married couples among them and about the depth of grief when one member of the couple must endure the loss of the other.

She also writes about dementia and nursing homes and funerals and the financial burdens of long-term care—all the realities avoided in the books about successful aging. Most of the events in the lives of her aging characters are tragic, but the stories are tragicomedies. Gallant is always aware of the simultaneous existence of pain and absurdity and she keeps a perfect balance between the two in her sad, funny presentations of the characters and their encounters.

Russell Baker's column, the "Observer," a satirical examination of American society, appeared in the *New York Times* from July 16, 1962, to December 25, 1998. The last decade of the "Observer" was also the decade when the baby boomers reached fifty, and Baker's columns about the aging boomers were (and are) perfect antidotes to the lies and fantasies promulgated by the marketers of the "new old age."

Baker did more than amuse his readers by making fun of people's foibles; he also (to use a phrase that Baker used in his essay about the journalist Murray Kempton) "brought moral judgment to bear." His column "Intimations of Mortality" not only satirizes the modern

Introduction

pursuit of immortality through diet and exercise, it also attacks its implicit blame-the-victim message:

> As the years passed, it became increasingly obvious that if I died it would be my own fault. This saddened me. When I die I want people to commiserate. I want to hear them say, "What a pity," and, "It's a rotten shame that this sort of thing should happen to a fine person like you, even if you were a little corrupt." ... Lately, though ... what you're more likely to hear is: "Tough buns, sweetheart. If you'd watched your cholesterol, exercised an hour a day, stuffed down more fiber, supplemented your calcium intake and popped a daily aspirin, you wouldn't be spoiling everybody's day with that death rattle...."[10]

But Baker drops his joking tone and becomes serious, and angry, as he writes of "the hateful inhumanity of the modern attitude that lets the survivors make you feel guilty ... because you didn't follow a strict health regimen." In an earlier column on a different subject but about the same attitude, Baker had pointed out its moral implications: "To comfort ourselves with the illusion that we can beat the rules, we deny a just portion of compassion to the sick and the dying."[11]

This was also the decade when Baker turned sixty-five and he wrote columns spoofing his own aging and columns about his views in, and from, age. Near the end of the decade, Baker retired, ending his short, satirical columns in the *Times* and beginning his long, reflective essay-reviews in *The New York Review of Books*. Instead of inventing the fictitious characters who appeared as guests in his columns, he now created portraits of the real people who were the subjects of his essays. Among them are his portraits in old age of three notable Americans: Senator Robert Byrd, Joseph Mitchell, and William Shawn.

The chapters in this book are arranged in chronological order according to the birth dates of the writers. Each chapter begins with an overview of the writer's work, then focuses on the works written in, and about, old age. The interview that follows the chapter listens to the writer's personal reflections on the subject.

1

V. S. Pritchett

V. S. Pritchett, who died in 1997 at the age of ninety-six, was the last of his kind, a great "man of letters" at the end of a long tradition in English writing that began with Samuel Johnson. Pritchett described the tradition in *Midnight Oil*, his memoir at seventy: "We have no captive audience. We do not teach. We write to be readable and to engage the interest of the 'common reader'" (the phrase was Dr. Johnson's). In a career of unflagging productivity that spanned more than six decades, Pritchett published eleven collections of short stories, nine volumes of literary criticism, three memoirs, three literary biographies, seven volumes of travel writing, and five novels (after 1951 he confined his fiction to the shorter form of the story).

I first discovered Pritchett when I was browsing through the shelves of my university library and came across *The Living Novel*, a collection of his literary essays. When I raved about it to a professor of English, I quickly realized that this was my second breach of etiquette as a doctoral student (the first was that I was a middle-aged woman). The professor dismissed Pritchett's criticism as biographical and impressionistic, lacking the "critical theory" that was de rigueur in English departments.

But I decided that because I *was* a middle-aged woman, studying literature for pleasure rather than for admission to the inner circles of academe, I would stay clear of the departmental dogmas of deconstruction, structuralism, poststructuralism et al., and the jargon-choked prose that went with them. I preferred Pritchett: unobtrusively erudite and passionately engaged with literature, not with academic argument. Besides, I found the biographical aspect of his criticism helpful: it showed the relationship between the writer's world and his writing, instead of narrowing the writing to a "text" to be parsed according to the critical methodology du jour.[1]

Another reason for the academic snootiness about Pritchett was that he lacked the formal credentials to certify him worthy of teaching in a university. His family's financial circumstances had forced him to leave school on his sixteenth birthday and he was sent to work in a leather factory in London. But, a voracious reader since early childhood, Pritchett continued to read and to educate himself. At twenty, he moved to Paris, where he spent his days as a photographer's assistant and a glue-and-shellac salesman, his nights teaching himself foreign languages (he became fluent in French and Spanish), and his weekends walking long distances and writing about what he saw.

Those early sketches landed him his first job in journalism as the *Christian Science Monitor*'s correspondent in Ireland, then in Spain. In 1928, at the age of twenty-eight, Pritchett published his first book, *Marching Spain*, and joined the *New Statesman* as a book reviewer and literary editor. During the Second World War, when the younger writers were called into the service, it fell to Pritchett to write the journal's weekly "Books in General." Few new books were being published and so Pritchett wrote his 2,000-word essays on classic works of English, European, American, and Latin American literature, which became the foundation of his monumental body of literary criticism.

On almost every page of Pritchett's literary essays and short stories you are stopped short by a sentence or phrase, not only because of the beauty of the language but because of how it swiftly illuminates a character, real or fictional—like Dostoyevsky, of whom Pritchett wrote, "Life stories of endless complexity hang shamelessly out of the mouths of his characters, like dogs' tongues, as they run by,"[2] or like the rich, aggrieved widow in his story "Tea with Mrs. Bittell," who sits in her flat "in the expensive block nearly opposite the church, among the wrongs and relics of her seventy years."[3]

People fascinated Pritchett, whether they were the authors in his essays or the characters in his stories. He populated his fictional world with shopkeepers and salesmen, clerks and bus drivers, hairdressers and housewives, and other members of the English lower-middle class, ordinary people going about the comedies and dramas of their daily lives. Many of the characters are foolish or eccentric, but Pritchett never ridiculed or patronized them: he *became* them.

In his essay on the nineteenth-century Spanish novelist Benito

Pérez Galdós, Pritchett could have been—indeed, may have been—writing about himself: "His intimacy with every social group is never the sociologist's; it is the personal intimacy of the artist; indeed it can be said he disappears as a person and becomes the people," Pritchett wrote. "The secret of his gift lies, I think, in his timing, his leisurely precision and above all in his ear for dialogue: his people live in speech.... What is more important is his ability to ... follow the feelings of his people with a tolerant and warm detachment." And then this concluding line of his essay, which captures perfectly Pritchett's own attitude toward his characters, those he observed and those he invented: "The fact is that Galdós accepts human nature without resentment."[4]

On Growing Old

Pritchett wrote about old age—his own and others'—in three of the many literary forms he mastered over his long career: the memoir, the literary essay, and the short story.

Memoirs

MIDNIGHT OIL

Pritchett begins *Midnight Oil* with an announcement: "This is the year of my seventieth birthday, a fact that bewilders me. I find it hard to believe. I understand now the look of affront I often saw in my father's face after this age and that I see in the faces of my contemporaries. We are affronted because, whatever we may feel, time has turned us into curiosities in some secondhand shop."[5]

He continues: "I have before me two photographs. One is, I regret, instantly recognizable: a bald man, sitting before a pastry board propped on a table, and writing. He does little else besides sit and write. His fattish face is supported by a valence of chins; the head is held together by glasses that slip down a bridgeless nose...." The other photograph, taken fifty years earlier, is of a "young fellow sitting on the table of a photographer's in Paris, a thin youth of twenty with thick fairish hair, exclaiming eyebrows, loosely grinning mouth and the eyes raised to the ceiling with a look of passing schoolboy saintliness.... The two, if they could meet in the flesh, would be stupefied, and," he adds, "the older one, would certainly be embarrassed" (217).

In addition to an amusing juxtaposition of Pritchett's younger and older selves, the opening provides a transition with his earlier coming-of-age memoir, *A Cab at the Door*, which ended as the youth of twenty was about to leave England for Paris. And the closing line of that memoir, "I became a foreigner. For myself that is what a writer is—a man living on the other side of a frontier," became Pritchett's personal and enduring metaphor for his vocation.[6]

In *Midnight Oil*, Pritchett picks up where *A Cab at the Door* left off and doesn't return to his seventy-year-old self until the final pages of the book, when, after describing his father's old age and death, he writes, "Now, in my turn, I have become an old man.... I am seventy, and in my father's phrase, 'I would like a little more.'" He points out that "one's age goes up and down ... all one's life. I shall never be as old as I was between twenty and thirty, when, with its deceitful energy, my young body carried a pained, fogged and elderly mind across France, Ireland, Spain and the Tennessee mountains on foot" (431).

Pritchett was referring to his long-distance walks, undertaken on his own in France, then as a correspondent for the *Christian Science Monitor*. And what rejuvenated his "elderly mind" at thirty was the *coup de foudre* that hit him when he met Dorothy Roberts, the young woman who would become his second wife. Pritchett had married an Irish actress, the marriage had failed, and they had separated. He "wondered if I should ever be fully in love" and decided that he "was one of those who must wait for the *coup de foudre*. Better the certainty of instinct than the muddle of too much thought," was his romantic conclusion (391).

"The *coup* came, of course," Pritchett tells us. He knew very little about Dorothy Roberts the first time she came to his studio, but "I loved instantly the voice and the way she laughed" (394). That evening "was appropriately Guy Fawkes Night with the London sky starred by rockets." Two years later, in 1936, when the divorce from his first wife came through, he and Dorothy married. It was a happy union that produced a daughter and a son and that lasted for sixty-one years until Pritchett's death.

But, as the title of this memoir suggests, the principal subject of *Midnight Oil* is how Pritchett became a writer, one "who spends his time becoming other people and places ... [and] finds he has written his life away and has become almost nothing" (217). If this description of his profession sounds rueful, Pritchett dispels that notion a little later in the book when he writes that he became "fanatical about writing: the word and the sentence were my religion" (382). And on the last page of *Midnight Oil*, after summing up a writer's life as mostly hard work, Pritchett explains that, for a writer or any artist, "leisure does not consist of lying on beaches in the Caribbean, but in a labour delightful because it is fanatical" (432).

As Old as the Century

Ten years after declaring in *Midnight Oil* that time had turned him and others of his age into "curiosities in some second-hand shop," Pritchett pointed out in *As Old as the Century*, a memoir for his eightieth birthday, that, because of the enormous increase in life expectancy, "the old are no longer revered curiosities...."

> We swarm in cities and resorts, ancient mariners who square our shoulders as we pick one another out at a glance in the pubs, the shops, the park seats, the planes and the tourist buses.... Not a day's illness—we boast—except a winter cough or a twinge of arthritis or gout; we speak of these twinges as medals we have won. Smoke like fish (we go on), drink like a chimney, pity people who do not work a twelve-hour day.... And as for this new thing called sex...! [*Pritchett's ellipsis*].[7]

He admits that this "acting" is "a defense against our fear of senility and death." Writing at eighty, Pritchett wonders, as all old people must, what will we be like "in our nineties? Are we for the old folks' home?" And he closes with the fear that haunts the old, who "have seen so many of our friends paralyzed, collapsing in mind and physically humiliated. Shall we escape?" (33).

Pritchett describes his appearance at eighty. "My hair is white now. Veins stand out on my temples, I have dark brown spots on my hands, my arms shrink, but in my mind I seem to be much what I was at fifty" (33). But, he says, "age is relative. At fifty-seven, I looked despairingly bleak, ill and flaccid, to judge from a photograph, less brisk than I became in my sixties, seventies or today." Reiterating his belief in the connection between passionate love and creative power, Pritchett writes that he was "far, far younger in my thirties than ... in my twenties," thanks to the *coup de foudre* that "pulled my scattered wits together" (34).

As Old as the Century (the title refers to his birth in the first year of the twentieth century) is a happy self-portrait of Pritchett at eighty and, for the man who described himself in *Midnight Oil* as "fanatical about writing," a necessary component of this happiness is his continuing ability to write. At eighty, he still goes "fast up the four flights of steep stairs to my study ... every day of the week, at nine o'clock in the morning, Saturdays and Sundays included ... groaning at the work I have to do, crying out dishonestly for leisure, ... complaining that surely at my age I should be able to get some time off" (34).

But, as soon as he has cleaned his pipe and "put my pen to paper," Pritchett is "under the spell of language which has ruled me since I was ten. A few minutes later—four hours' writing have washed out all sense of time—my wife calls me down to a delicious lunch. She has spent the morning typing what I wrote the day before ... and knowing she'll have to do the whole damn thing over again two or three times because I cover each page with an ant's colony of corrections; she is a perfectionist too" (34).

After lunch and an hour's nap, he goes out to do some household errands in neighboring Camden Town, "where I pass as an old pensioner called Pritchard," and at four-o'clock returns home for tea. It sounds like a typical afternoon in the life of a retired Englishman, except that Pritchett takes his cup of tea up to his study and writes for another three hours. At seven o'clock, he joins his wife for a drink and dinner; after dinner he catches up with correspondence or, if the weather is fine, works in the garden. By ten, they are in bed, where Pritchett "dreams wildly" and sometimes goes on writing in his sleep, "in English mostly but often, out of vanity, in Spanish or French" (35).

"I am a very lucky man, of course," he says (35). Lucky to be able to work at home, lucky to be able to earn his living as a writer, "which I dreamed of when I was a boy,'" lucky "to be 'in work,'" and not, like "many a pensioner, forced to be idle against his will" (36). He quotes Thomas Hardy, who in his old age said that "to write poetry was simply a matter of physical strength." "So is writing prose," Pritchett says, and quotes Keats, who said that "work makes 'the disagreeables evaporate'" (36).

Then, in three pages of economical but leisurely prose, Pritchett covers the first forty years of his life, beginning with his boyhood in Edwardian London, delightfully evoked through his sense of smell: "I coughed my way through a city stinking, rather excitingly, of coal smoke, gas escapes, tanyards, breweries, horse manure and urine.... The streets smelled of beer; men and boys reeked of hair oil, vaseline, strong tobacco, powerful boot polish.... The smell of women was racy and scented" (37).

The end of World War I liberated him from his job in the leather factory and from "the hurdles of the then sticky English class system." Travel was cheap and he went to France and "discovered I could write sketches. I became the autodidact abroad and education was open to me at last" (38). Since then, "my life ... as a writer has been spent on crossing and recrossing frontiers," he writes, repeating his lifelong metaphor for his profession. The famously cheerful Pritchett doesn't complain that age has placed restrictions on the travel that had been an integral part of his writing life; instead he writes, "It cheers me that I live on the frontier of Camden Town and Regent's Park" (39).

All the same, an uncharacteristically dark note enters this memoir. "At eighty I look at the horrible state of our civilization," he writes. "It seems to be breaking up and returning to the bloody world of Shakespeare's Histories, which we thought we had outgrown.... We have now to school ourselves to deal with danger and tragedy" (43). But then he refers to an eighty-six-year-old friend, recently hit by a tragedy in his family, who "said he wanted to die at once—but not, he added, until he had seen what happened next in Poland and after that in Iran" (44). At eighty, Pritchett, too, is sustained by his curiosity.

As for the alleged wisdom and serenity of old age, Pritchett doesn't know if he is wiser, but he is more tolerant than when he was young. Serenity in old men "is more often torpor and I am drawn to activity and using myself. And to laughter, which wakes up the mind." The pleasures of old age are of "the lingering kind," and love "becomes more mysterious, tender and lasting." For Pritchett, "the great distress of old age" is "the death of friends, the thinning ranks of one's generation.... Something of oneself is drained away when friends go..." (45).

Among the old, he notes, "the new sensation is that living people are a wonder. Have you noticed how old people stare at groups of talkers, as if ... joining them silently at a distance?" Then he adds, perhaps with a bit of justified pride, that "this does not happen to me much for I am always on the move." Still, knowing that his time is limited, he finds himself "looking at streets and their architecture much longer and more intensely and at Nature and landscape. I gaze at the plane tree at the end of the garden, studying its branches and its leaves.... And I am always on the watch for the dramatic changes in the London sky" (46).

"I have no religious faith," Pritchett writes. "I am no pantheist or sentimentalist in my love of nature." But, he adds, "I came across a line by Camus which drily describes people like myself: 'One of our contemporaries is cured of his torment simply by contemplating a landscape.' That and lately falling into the habit of reading Gibbon's *Decline and Fall* on Sunday evenings, evaporates the 'disagreeables' of history that now advance on us" (46–7).

Literary Essays

"Growing Old"

Pritchett's ability to transform the genre of the book review into the more reflective genre of the literary essay is evident in his essay-reviews of two books about growing old: *The Coming of Age*, by Simone de Beauvoir and *The View in Winter*, by Ronald Blythe. As a reviewer, Pritchett discusses the books and, as an essayist, he uses them as springboards for his own explorations of the subject. It's significant that these books were written by literary figures—Beauvoir, the French writer and philosopher, and Blythe, the English essayist and editor. It is unlikely that Pritchett would have reviewed a book by a social scientist or any other "expert" on old age.

Indeed, in "Growing Old," his review of Beauvoir's book, Pritchett notes that Samuel Beckett, in his trilogy of novels about old age, *Molloy, Malone Dies,* and *The Unnamable,* "shows how artists are more sensitive to the burning theme that is hidden or repressed in any given period than the sociologists or reformers are. And indeed see it sooner." I would add that Pritchett shows how a literary critic, who is also an artist, is sensitive to the hidden themes of a novelist. Beckett's old men and old women, he notes, "are at war not with death but with their own vitality. His old people are agonized by the life force that prevents them from dying."[8]

Beauvoir's *The Coming of Age* (the original French title was the uneuphemized *La Vieillesse* [*Old Age*]) is a sweeping investigation of old age through the centuries, beginning in primitive societies and continuing, epoch by epoch, from the Greeks and Romans up to the latter part of the twentieth century. Her object, Pritchett says, "is to break the conspiracy of silence on a subject that has become privately and publicly taboo in the advanced countries which are governed by the values of profit-making capitalism" (1107).

Pritchett did not share Beauvoir's Marxist beliefs, but he shared her indignation that "old age has become the scrap heap," and he emphasizes the irony that "the percentage of elderly people in the wealthier and more advanced countries has enormously increased since the beginning of the century. All but a few are forced to end what sentimental liars have called 'the golden years' on declining means among the middle class, and in poverty ... among the workers" (1107). He wrote this essay when pensions were meager, but he also pointed out that "the real shock" of retirement "lies in being disqualified" (1109).

Pritchett's view of what we now call "gender roles" was a traditional one, so that when he describes the negative psychological effects of retirement (which he calls "the modern nightmare"), he is writing about men: "Some recover, others fall into poor health and listlessness when work stops. In all countries a very large proportion of the retired men simply hang about the house, particularly in America" (1109). His observation about retired men in America was acute—and prescient: more than three decades later, it remains a frequent complaint of their wives.

"One would have expected a writer with a Marxist turn of mind to make the Communist practices clearer and, above all, more living than they appear here," Pritchett observes of Beauvoir, in a mild but, for him, rare criticism of another writer's style (1108). He concedes that "one is obviously better off in these countries if one belongs to the Party," but, he says, he is opposed to the establishment of "'old-folks' communities" and depressed by "the unnatural sight of people living entirely and perforce among people of their own age." He has visited such places, Pritchett says, and his objections sound more visceral than philosophical when he recalls "the stiff, lifeless rooms" where "the smell of old age pervades" (1108).

Beauvoir is "on more certain ground when she writes about old age as it affects us privately," he writes, especially when she challenges the "conspiracy to make us believe that the old are different from ourselves" (1111). (It's worth noting that Pritchett, who wrote this essay one month before his seventy-first birthday, refers to the old as different from "*ourselves*.") "Their passions, their sexuality, their needs are intensified by the discovery that all time does not stretch before them.... As [Beauvoir] says, there is a return not to second childhood but to something like the willfulness of children, and if old people are strange it is because, as ... the Greek tragedians saw, there is a psychological reconnection with the fantasies of childhood and adolescence" (1111).

"If life is tragic," he continues, "society takes the view of comedy: the sexuality of old people is frequently laughed at or censured..." (1111). The sexual antics of old men and old women were a staple of satire and, as a literary critic, Pritchett acknowledges that "the comedy of disgust is as much a purgation as tragedy is." But "to censure elderly sexuality is to forget that in those who have had a rich sexual life, it will be prolonged." And he repeats his conviction that sexuality is "at the heart of the creative imagination, whether in artists or in the ordinary man" (1111).

"What is difficult for the old is sexual loneliness," Pritchett continues. "It is much worse for older women than for men, though I cannot agree with Mlle de Beauvoir that no one speaks of 'a beautiful old woman.' In any case, instinctive sexual attraction may not depend on beauty at all. A voice, for example, is as potent as a body" (1111). And here we remember Pritchett's writing in *Midnight Oil* that when he met Dorothy, the woman who would become his second wife, he "loved instantly the voice and the way she laughed."[9]

At the conclusion of the essay, Pritchett departs from Beauvoir's book and writes a personal meditation on old age, which begins on a cheerful note and ends with a poignant observation about the death of friends as the "great distress of old age":

> If we are not struck by mortal disease many of us in our seventies nowadays feel little different from what we were at fifty ... except that we now know time is shorter. If by luck of vocation or temperament we are incurably active we have little time to think of our decline. But our sense of the mysteriousness of life becomes sharper and we are jarred by the death of friends.... If we are vain of our survival we now discover a more piercing grief, for the dead have taken away a part of ourselves. Indeed, it might be said that what the old learn at last is how to grieve [1114].

But then he adds a buoyant paragraph about old age at its best and, for Pritchett, old age at its best is "unresting":

> We all have known ... men and women ... in their eighties and nineties who are incredibly clear in mind and vibrating with life ... and if they have their aches and pains, they have added to their lives by increasing their work and not by rest. Perhaps they were born unresting [1114].

"Finite Variety"

In *The View in Winter,* Ronald Blythe studied old age in twentieth-century England, specifically the old age of the residents of an English village that he called Akenfield. The book begins with Blythe's essay on old age, interwoven with apposite selections from literary works. The succeeding chapters consist of his interviews with the elderly villagers, deftly shaped into stories and accompanied by the author's observations and reflections. One would expect that Pritchett, a storyteller himself and a writer who believed that the truth was more likely to be revealed in the specific example than in the broad generalization, would find Blythe's approach to the subject of old age more congenial than Beauvoir's, and so he suggests in this description:

> Mr. Blythe's book is neither a clinical nor a statistical social study. He has read his Simone de Beauvoir, but he is not as tendentious as she was. His book is essentially an unflinching, inquiring, and reflective essay, graced by wide reading of the poets, novelists, and philosophers and brought sharply to life by interviews in which the old ... talk about their experience and their dreads.[10]

Pointing out that the increase in life expectancy is the underlying theme of Blythe's book, Pritchett begins his essay with a sobering consideration of this phenomenon. "We are almost a new species," he declares, and then explains that what makes us almost a new species is not that we will live much longer, but that we will be old much longer:

> How is it that we seventy- and eighty-year-olds still frostily survive? Death we know comes to everyone, but what about great length of life? Once the odds were short but now in our generation they have lengthened in our favor—if that is the word—of long life. In Western societies the *average* expectation of life has jumped from forty years to more than seventy; nothing like this has been known in human history. We are almost a new species. Most of us have to face the prospect of a long old age before we die....

He gives brief descriptions of the people in Blythe's interviews—"the old cottager, farmer, miner, the matron, the nurse, ... the survivors of that almost extinct 'brotherhood,' the men who fought in the 1914 war, an engineer, a senior neurologist, an actor, many widows and priests...." Most of them are cheerful, Pritchett notes, with the exception of the neurologist, who has discovered "the slowing down of his own intellect and the failure (so common in writers) to do more than rewrite his old ideas."

After the parenthetical comment that seems to suggest a parallel between the aging neurologist and the aging writer, Pritchett points out that the difference between the two is the "creative or imaginative gift that survives in artists," which is a "fortification even when talent is condemned to repeat itself." And, as he had done in his review of Beauvoir's book, Pritchett condemns the practice of compulsory retirement:

> The chief peril we full-timers have to face is ... retirement ... for we are sustained by the discipline of work, which is a sensual energy. Retirement is a great evil; purpose and authority are snatched from those who retire. The happiest are those in trades and professions, or the self-employed who are lucky enough to be able to work until the end....

Like Beauvoir, Blythe writes about the taboo of sex in old age, and Pritchett leads into—or backs into—that subject with his observation that, since the establishment of the welfare state in Britain, the population of the old has seen "startling improvement in their material lot.... The traditional dread of the work house has long gone." But, he writes, "what they want is what they have had. They desire."

Pritchett summarizes Blythe's description of the attitudes of the young and the middle-aged to sexuality in the old. They are the ones who "decide what is unbecoming in the old, and not the old who feel it." They assure the old that they naturally become asexual and that, if they do not conform to that expectation, they will be "ludicrous or indecent." In a reversal of roles, the middle-aged children "lay down the rules of proper sexual behavior to their elderly parents," who "have to pretend to a seemliness they do not feel.... All passion is not spent at seventy or eighty," Pritchett writes, "but it pays the old to behave as if it were so."

At the end of his essay-review praising Blythe's book, Pritchett says that the one thing he missed was "an examination of the sadistic rages and hysterical fantasies that many of us old people are subject to, especially as the new world outside becomes a jungle of terrorism, massacre, and violence in the streets." (It was that violent new world that Pritchett wrote about the following year in his memoir *As Old as the Century*.) The other thing he missed, Pritchett adds, is "that tolerant delight in the follies of their friends which seems to me to have increased among my fellow irascibles. The elderly are usually aware of the comedy of their condition."

Stories

"The Spree"

"The Spree," Pritchett's great comic story about grief, demonstrates his ability to inhabit his characters, a process that he called "unselfing," which enabled him to speak for those unable to speak for themselves. "The Spree" is written from the protagonist's point of view and in the protagonist's voice, but also, with a self-effacement that approaches invisibility, in the humane and gently ironic voice of the author.

The story takes place over the course of one day, during which the protagonist, a seventy-year-old widower and retired commercial traveler, goes to London for a haircut, then takes a bus to the seaside town of

Brighton: an ordinary day in the life of an ordinary man. But because Pritchett writes from deep inside his character, he also reveals the dreams and dramas of his inner life and the pathos beneath his comic surface.

Pritchett introduces his protagonist—he calls him only "the old man," perhaps to suggest his loss of a sense of identity in old age—in the opening sentences, which tell us that the sensual enjoyment of his conjugal bed now exists only in the old man's dreams, whose abrupt endings return him to his bereaved state:

> The old man—but when does old age begin?—the old man turned over in bed and putting out his hand to the crest of his wife's beautifully white rising hip and comforting bottom, hit the wall with his knuckles and woke up. More than once during the two years since she had died he had done this....[11]

As he begins his morning ablutions, he looks in the mirror "indignantly," an apt word to describe an old man's reaction to his age-altered reflection (it reminds us of Pritchett's look of "affront" at his own aging face in *Midnight Oil*). But the loss of his looks (and his teeth) is dwarfed by his other losses: "It was awful to think, as he put his teeth in to cover the horror of his mouth, that twelve or fourteen hours of London daylight were stacked up meaninglessly waiting for him" (396). Retired, he has lost his sense of purpose.

He has also lost his independence, a matter that he addresses in an imaginary speech to his son, whispered into his towel: "I'm not saying I'm ungrateful. But old and young are not meant to be together. You've got your life. I've got mine. The children are sweet—you're too sharp with them—but I can't stand the noise. I don't want to live at your expense. I want a place of my own. Where I can breathe. Like Frenchy" (396).

Pritchett has unobtrusively inserted two important aspects of the old man's character. He is bossy (even in an imaginary speech to his son, he can't resist the impulse to correct him) and, like so many of the characters in Pritchett's stories, he is a fantasist. His current fantasy is to emulate Frenchy, his dentist, who, like himself, is "seventy if he was a day," and who has bought a small house by the sea. "Get a house by the sea," Frenchy told him on his last visit. "It keeps you young" (396). The dentist's idly dropped remark has ignited the old man's imagination.

His silent speech to his son is also a cry of frustration from a man whom old age has robbed of his wife, his house in London, and his privacy—a frustration that reaches its peak when his daughter-in-law comes into his room, "like a soft Jersey cow with eyes too big and reproachful ... bringing him tea, the dear sweet tiresome woman" (396). The tea, which is "not like the tea he used to make for his wife when she was alive but had too much milk in it, always tepid, left standing somewhere," is the objective correlative for his losses.

In a theatrical gesture, he holds his hairbrush high and, "asserting his right to live, to get out of the house, in air he could breathe," he announces to his daughter-in-law, "'I'm going into London to get my hair cut.' ... For the old man it was not a mere scissoring and clipping of the hair. It was a ceremonial of freedom; it had the whiff of orgy, the incitement of a ritual. As the years went by, leaving him in such a financial mess that he was now down to not much more than a pension, it signified desire" (396–7).

He is, after all, a sensual old man who dreams of his late wife's comforting bottom and is instantly "intoxicated" by the scent of the rose he plucks from his son's garden for his buttonhole (397). As he waits in the queue for the bus to London, his thoughts reveal that his present financial mess is the result of his past extravagances: "Times have changed," he laments. "Before I retired, when Kate was alive—though I must honestly say we often had words about it—I always took a cab" (397).

The bus deposits him at his "temple—the most expensive of the big shops," and Pritchett's description of his tour of the store is as exact as a map of Harrods perceived through the old man's senses, aroused by the aphrodisiac of wealth (397). "Reborn on miles of carpet" and "inflamed by hall after hall of women's dresses and hats, ... he passed into the echoing hall of provisions. He saw the game, the salmon, and the cheese ... and moved on to lose twenty years in the men's clothing department where, among ties and brilliant shirts ... his ears heard the voices of the rich" (397).

Revived by his contact with luxury, he descends the oak steps to the barbershop and to the enactment of the funny, painful scene that dramatizes his greatest loss: his identity. The shop is empty and the barbers are standing around in a group, chatting. One of them seats the old man and puts a cape on him; then, taking a few steps back toward the others, calls out, "He wasn't at the staff meeting." The old man "tapped his finger irritably under his sheet. Barbers did not cut hair, it seemed. They went to staff meetings.... 'Where is Charles?' said the old man to call the barbers to order.... 'Charles?' said the barber. 'Yes. Charles. He shaved me for twenty years.' 'He retired.' Another emptiness, another cavern, opened inside the old man" (397).

Although his head was being washed in lotions and oils, the old man noticed that the place, which in days gone by, "had been baronial, now ... seemed not quite to gleam. One could not be a sultan among a miserable remnant of men who held staff meetings" (398). And when he leaves, the woman who takes his money keeps talking on the phone and does not know his name.

What strikes the old man as he steps out of the shop, is that he was "cool, scented, and light-headed ... ready for anything—but cut off from expectancy, unknown nowadays to anybody, free for nothing" (398). He has become anonymous, purposeless and, perhaps worst of all, "cut off from expectancy": in old age, he no longer has anything to look forward to. But, with a combination of pluck and bravado, he admonishes himself not "to fall into that trap: old people live in the past. And I am not old. Old I am not!" (398).

Pulling himself together, he retraces his former routes to the shops "which had bought his goods years ago ... and where he knew no one now," and to the café, "which had changed its décor" (398). Even the dream on which he had always drawn for consolation has dissolved: "He with his appetite for everything, who could not pass a shop window, or an estate agent's, or a fine house, without greed watering in his mouth, could buy nothing. He hadn't the cash" (398). That short last sentence and the monosyllabic finality of its last word emphasizes that the ability to spend money had been a crucial part of his identity.

Theatrical even in despair, the old man tells himself that he must now "drag his way to the inevitable bus stop of defeat, and stand, as so many Londoners did, with surrender on their faces" (399). Then, clutching at a final straw, he sees a phone booth and impulsively decides to call his dentist, Frenchy. A child answers and he realizes that he has not dialed Frenchy's number but the number of his old house, "the one he had sold after Kate died" (399). For the first time, he is frightened that his mind is beginning to go. "Tottering with horror" he backs out of the phone booth and edges his way along the wall to the neighboring pub, where he leans weakly against the doorway (399).

And at this most desperate point, Pritchett stages one of his great crowd scenes, which provides an exhilarating contrast to the atmosphere of loneliness and solitude that has permeated the first part of the story. Pushed through the door into the pub by a crowd of young people on a company excursion, the old man, taken for a retired member of the firm, is given a glass of brandy, then another, then is pushed again out into the street and to the steps of the waiting bus. He tries to make himself heard over the clamor and confusion, to explain that a mistake has been made. Suddenly, everything changes when he sees this glorious comic vision:

> A woman wearing a flowered dress with a red belt, a woman as stout as himself had a foot on the step of the bus and was trying to heave herself up while people in front of her blocked the door. She nearly fell. The old man, all smiles and sadness, put on a dignified anger. He pushed his way towards her. He turned forbiddingly on the youngsters. "Allow me, madam," he said, and took the woman's cool fat elbow and helped her up the step, putting his own foot on the lower one [401].

Pushed again, this time into the bus, he struggles to get out, but the driver tells him to sit down and the old man, "for the first time in his adult life, indignantly obeyed an order" (402). Before long he is asleep and snoring and dreaming his tragicomic dreams (there are three of them in the story, each with a whiff of death) and when he wakes up, the bus has stopped. It is empty except for the stout woman, who tells him that the bus broke down and all the young people got off. "They've got to send another coach. Don't you move until it comes," she instructs him (404).

The old man knows that he must find a train or another bus to get home, "but since his wife had died he had never been as near to a strange woman's face.... It was less the nearness of the face than her voice that kept him there" (404). His thoughts about her voice lead to a brief meditation on her breasts and end in a comic fantasy of power:

> It came out in deep breaths drawn up from soft but heavy breasts that could, he imagined, kick up a hullabaloo, a voice which suggested that

… she would say whatever came into her head. It was the kind of voice that made the old man swell with a polite, immensely intimate desire to knock the nonsense out of her [405].

Through the woman's silent appraisal, and in just once sentence, Pritchett gives a picture of the old man that suggests his sartorial extravagances and his roguish appeal: "He stood with a plump man's dignity, but what saved him in her eyes were his smart, well-cut clothes, his trim hair, and the jaunty rose: he looked like an old rip, a racing man—possibly a crook—at any rate, a bit of a rogue on the spree, yet innocent too" (406).

Their ensuing conversation, conducted in counterpoint with their unspoken thoughts as they size each other up, is a masterpiece of comic dialogue that leads to the most gripping part of the story. The woman tells him that her late husband was a member of the board of the company; the old man tells her that he has retired from the company. She tells him that she has a house by the sea that she's thinking of selling; he tells her that he is thinking of buying one. Then he admits that he is not a retired member of the company and that he got on the bus just for the ride. "No one checked?" she asks, shocked. "No one checked," he answers, thinking, "it was a definition of paradise" (406).

Finally, he confides to her that by mistake, he had phoned the house he used to live in, "where Kate—when my wife—was alive" and that, when a girl answered, "I thought my mind had gone. I thought, I really did think, for a second, it was my wife." The woman asks him when his wife died and, when he tells her it was two years ago, she says, "It was grief. That is what it was—grief" (407). The word strikes him with the force of a revelation and prompts his reflections on grief in a passage that is a seamless blend of Pritchett's language and the old man's loneliness:

> Grief. Yes, it was. He blinked away the threat of tears before her understanding. In these two years he seemed … to be dragging an increasing load of unsaid things behind him, things he had no one to tell. With his son and his daughter-in-law and their young friends he sat with his mouth open ready to speak, but he could never get a word out.… What he needed was not friends, for since so many friends had died he had become a stranger; he needed another stranger. Perhaps like this woman … [who] if not as old as he was had joined his lonely race and had the lost look of going nowhere.… Grief—what was it—a craving. Yet not for

a face or even a voice or even for love, but for a body. But dressed. Say in a flowered dress [408].

When a second bus arrives to take the passengers to their party in Brighton, the woman suggests that they go to her house instead. He can ring his son from there and take a look at the house, she says; he might buy it. They get into her parked car and she drives him to "one of the ugliest bungalows he had ever seen" (412). This first impression is followed, when they go inside, by his silent assessment of tasks to be done: "Pull down a few walls, reface the front, move out the furniture ... that's what you'd have to do..." (412).

But his mood sours when the woman tells him that she wants thirty-one thousand pounds for the house. "The sum was so preposterous that it ... made him spill his tea in his saucer. 'If I decide to sell,' she said, noticing his shock. 'If anyone offers you that,' he said dryly, 'I advise you to jump at it.' They regarded each other with disappointment" (412–13).

When she drives him to the train station, she takes the long way, "and there indeed was the sea, the real sea.... He liked being with the woman in the car [and] he was sad his day was ending. 'I feel better,' she said. 'I think I'll go [to the party] after all,' she said, watching him. 'I feel like a spree.' But he did not rise. 'Thirty-one thousand!' he thought. 'The ideas women have!'" (413)

"At the station they shook hands and she said, 'Next time you come to Brighton' ... [Pritchett's ellipsis] and she touched his rose with her finger. The rose was drooping. He got on the train" (413). Those three sentences, including the reference to the flower that he had picked that morning, suggest that the old man's feelings of bereavement have not been ameliorated by his encounter with the woman.

A brief coda leaves the story's conclusion unresolved. " 'Who is this lady friend who keeps ringing you up from Brighton?' ... [his daughter-in-law] asked in her lowing voice several times in the following weeks. [The lowing voice reminds us of the old man's earlier comparison of his daughter-in-law to a Jersey cow.] 'A couple I met at Frenchy's,' he said on the spur of the moment.... I might go down to see them next week ... Frenchy's heard of a house.'" He enjoys teasing her but, as Pritchett writes in the suggestive but enigmatic closing sentence, "The old man knew that what he needed was not a house" (413).

In this portrait of the old man, Pritchett shows all his flaws: he is foolish, pompous, egocentric, financially irresponsible, and occasionally absurd. But Pritchett also shows his courage, his imagination, and his dogged refusal to give in to self-pity or defeat. Above all, he takes him seriously and we are persuaded to do the same.

"On the Edge of the Cliff"

The protagonist of "On the Edge of the Cliff," another seventy-year-old retired widower, is nothing like "the old man" in "The Spree." Harry, a former university professor, shares his house in a Welsh village with the woman he loves, Rowena, a painter in her twenties, who adores him. Pritchett never airbrushes his portrait of Harry to make him a more plausible object of a young woman's desire; he shows his quirks and habits associated with old age.

For example, Harry is fussy and set in his ways: "It was his house, not hers. He'd lived alone long enough not to be able to stand a woman in his kitchen, could not bear to see [Rowena] cut a loaf or muddle the knives and forks or choke the sink with tea leaves."[12] He also tends to talk "nonstop about prehistoric civilizations or the lives of plants," although he tries to keep in mind that "at this age one had to avoid repeating oneself if possible" (459).

But Harry has the erudition and intellectual sophistication that is attractive to a young woman like Rowena, who has artistic and literary aspirations of her own. And he has the charm and assurance of a former ladies' man, one of the details about his past that Pritchett reveals, bit by bit as the story unfolds, so that we discover Harry gradually, as we would in life. Harry can view his affair with Rowena, which is serious, with the irony that comes from experience: "There are rules for old men who are in love with young girls, all the stricter when the young girls are in love with them. It has to be played as a game" (459). And so he sometimes pretends to be jealous; and he refrains from saying anything that would draw attention to the great difference in their ages.

But Pritchett draws attention to that difference and at the same time suggests the piquant charm of their May-December relationship:

> While he fussed between the kitchen and the room they ate in, she came down late and idled, throwing back her long black hair, lassoing him

with smiles and side glances thrown out and rushed at him while he had a butter plate in his hand and gave him another of her light engulfing hugs and laughed at the plate he waved in the air [459].

Pritchett's stories characteristically focus on a particular event and in this story it is Harry and Rowena's climb to Withy Hole, a crater on the Welsh coast so deep that it can barely be seen from the edge of the highest cliff. It is Harry's favorite climb and Rowena's too, except for Withy Hole itself, which frightens her. First, though, she wants to stop at a country fair along the way and, although Harry regards the fair as "a cultural pathos" … "plastic, like cheap food," and another example of how "the twentieth century has packaged everything," he, as usual, indulges her (460).

The interlude at the fair emphasizes the disparity in their ages. As Harry watches Rowena go to the stalls, buy an ice cream cone, and ride on the roundabout, he reflects that the greatest difference between the young and the old is their attitude toward time: "In one's seventies, one is a miser of time, putting it by, hiding the minutes," while Rowena "spent fast, not knowing she was living in time at all" (460). And, although he watches Rowena with delight, "as she whirled round, a young miracle, getting younger and younger," he is aware of himself, "absurdly among the other patient watchers, older than all," and, in a particularly poignant observation about his old age, "all curiosity gone" (461).

Another of the watchers, a middle-aged woman who has been waving at a young man on the roundabout, approaches Harry. "'You don't remember me,' she accused him in a high voice" (461). He doesn't recognize her at first, but then "the hard little begging, pushing mouth and its high voice broke into his memory" (461). Her unexpected appearance angers him and precipitates a feeling of vulnerability that Pritchett suggests is peculiar to the old. (It's a highly articulate version of the old man's reaction to the barbershop in "The Spree"):

> What an appalling thing! But there it is—one must expect it when one is old: the map in one's head, indeed the literal map of the country empties and loses its contours, towns and villages, and people sink out of sight. The protective faces of friends vanish and one is suddenly alone, naked and exposed … and the enemy stands before one [462].

The "enemy" is Daisy Pyke, a woman who, decades earlier, had been in love with Harry and tried to make trouble between him and his late wife. He wants to rush off, but Rowena insists on being introduced to her. Harry muses that Rowena "was always eager to know, as if to possess, everyone he had ever known ... even the dead. Above all, Violet, his wife. Rowena longed to be as old as that dead woman" (463). Daisy, in turn, introduces the young man, Stephen, who had been on the roundabout and who, Harry assumes, is her son.

Pritchett, a meticulous craftsman, was always attentive to the construction of his stories, and the encounter with Daisy Pyke sets the plot in motion. But the real significance of the encounter is its effect on Harry, which is dramatized in the next scene, the climb to Withy Hole. When they start out, Harry is still grumbling about the "new, rootless civilization, anarchic but standardized" that he had observed at the fair (464). But as they climb higher, passing and leaving behind other signs of that civilization—the empty caravan sites, the sand dunes "dotted with last year's litter," the groups of surfers looking for bigger waves—and the sea appears below, "the old man was suddenly in command" (464). Suffocated by the vulgarity of the fair, the intrusion of Daisy Pyke, and the sense of time closing in on him, "that is what he had come for: boundlessness, distance" (464).

As they ascend, the prose also soars. In precisely observed detail, Pritchett evokes the stark beauty of the Welsh landscape and, without straining for symbolic equivalences, uses that landscape to deepen his portrait of Harry. At first Rowena looks at Harry with a young woman's romanticized view, comparing him to heroic figures—a "pagan saint" or a "prophet" (465). But when they reach Withy Hole, which terrifies Rowena and makes her think of "a great meaningless wound," her portrait of Harry contains images of old age and decay: "As he stood at the edge he seemed to her to be at one with it. It reminded her of his mouth when she had once seen it (with a horror she tried to wipe from her mind) before he put his dentures in" (465).

They find a spot to rest and sit in silence for a long time. Rowena breaks the silence when she asks Harry what he is thinking about. "He was going to say 'At my age one is always thinking about death,' but he said 'You,'" Pritchett writes, showing the intimations of mortality that are never far from an old person's mind. And Rowena's rejoinder, "You are a liar. You're thinking about Daisy Pike," reflects the half-teasing, half-jealous thoughts of a young woman, whose jealousy is not of Daisy, but of the years that Daisy knew Harry before Rowena was born. She persists. "Isn't the cove just below where you all used to bathe with nothing on? Did she come?" (466). Then, although Harry cautions her that it is too cold to swim, she runs barefoot to the edge of the sea. "'It's ice!' she screamed....

> But he was not there. He was out on the rocks, he had pulled off his clothes. He was standing there, his body furred with grey hair, his belly wrinkled, his thighs shrunk. Up went his bony arms. "You're not to! It will kill you! Your heart!" she shouted. He gave a wicked laugh, she saw his yellow teeth, and in he dived and was crawling and shouting in the water as he swam out farther, defying her, threshing the water, and then as she screamed at him, really frightened, he came crawling in like some ugly hairy sea animal, his skin reddened with cold, and stood dripping with his arms wide as if he was going to give a howl ... [466-7].

This unsparing picture of Harry brings to mind the "poor, bare, forked animal" in King Lear's description of man; but it has some of the king's grandeur in it too. Like Lear on the heath, Harry stands on the rocks naked, old, and vulnerable, but defiant in his rage against time and mortality.

That night Harry "could not sleep; he had broken one of his rules for old men. For the first time he had let her see him naked." But, although Rowena was frightened, she was not repelled, and the Withy Hole sequence ends with these tender lines: "He was astounded when she came into his room and got into his bed: she had not done this before. 'I've come to see the Ancient Mariner,' she said" (467).

The next day Daisy Pike pays a visit to Harry when Rowena is out. Certain that Daisy is after him and that she will make trouble with Rowena as she had with his wife, Harry is taken aback to learn that the purpose of her visit is to ask him to stay away. The young man on the roundabout was not Daisy's son, but her lover, and she points out to Harry that if the four of them spend any time together, their young lovers will be drawn to each other.

When Rowena comes home and he tells her that Stephen is Daisy's lover, she is shocked. "'You can't mean that,' she said.... She's old enough—' but she stopped, and ... rumpled his hair. 'People do confide in you, I must say,' she said. 'I don't think I like her coming up here. Tell me what she said'" (473). This closing section of the story has its ironies and, as always, Pritchett's beautiful sentences; but after the dramatic pitch of the Withy Hole scene, it is more like an epilogue than a final act.

"THE IMAGE TRADE"

A Careless Widow and Other Stories was published in Pritchett's eighty-ninth year and in "The Image Trade," the last story in his last book, Pritchett, who had always spoken for others, at last spoke for himself. The protagonist is a famous aging writer who lives in London and whose name—Pearson—and life are very much like his creator's. It is a wry self-portrait of the writer in old age.

One wonders what it was like for Pritchett to write a story about his writing life when he knew that it was coming to an end. But, like his other stories about old age, "The Image Trade" is a mixture of high spirits, irony, and an underlying awareness of mortality. And Pritchett, that most gregarious and least solipsistic of writers, adds two comic characters to enliven the story: Zut, the photographer, and Mrs. Zut, his wife and assistant.

"What do you make of the famous Zut—I mean his stuff in this exhibition?" Pearson asks the other passengers on the bus (silently) as they leave the opening of the photographer's show. "Is he just a newsy collector of human instances jellied in his dark room, or is he an artist ... searching another ... soul?"[13] A flashback then whisks us back to the day that Pearson sat for his photograph and to our first glimpse of Zut and Mrs. Zut through Pearson's eyes when he opens his front door. His brief, humorous observation reveals a great deal about Zut and his relationship with his wife: "There stood Zut, the photographer, with his back to Pearson and on impatient feet, tall and thin in a suit creased by years of air travel. He was shouting to Mrs. Zut, who was lugging two heavy bags of apparatus up the street to the house" (153).

Pearson makes fun of himself too, as "switching on an eager smile, [he] bowed them into the house" (154). Like a tour guide, he takes them through it, room by room, floor by floor, in search of a setting that will satisfy Zut's undivulged requirements. He accompanies his tour with a (silent) monologue, which is a satirical but accurate description of V. S.

Pritchett's house, his writing career, even his changes in appearance and clothing styles through six decades. Pearson's monologue becomes increasingly frantic as he struggles to break through Zut's unrelenting silence. ("Zut," a mild French expletive, is an inspired choice for the name of the laconic photographer, whose only utterances are the monosyllabic orders that he barks at his wife and at Pearson.)

Zut finally decides to photograph Pearson at the writing table in his fourth-floor study. "'There,' said Zut, pointing to the chair in front of it.... 'Sit,' he said.... 'Take your glasses off.... Don't smile.'" Pearson removes his glasses, but warns Zut, silently, "If you take me naked, you will miss all the *et cetera* of my life. I am all *et cetera*." Zut takes everything off Pearson's writing table, "and then he did something presumptuous. He ... moved a pot of pencils out of the way" (157–8). It was "the blue pot, that rather pretty *et cetera* that Pearson's wife had found in a junk shop next to the butcher's—now a pizza café—twenty-four years ago....

"Zut, you have moved part of my life to another table, it will hate being there, screamed Pearson's soul. How dare you move my wife?" (158). The blue pot, freighted with meaning as part of the old writer's past and a symbol of his wife, is, like all the ineffable *et ceteras* that make up a life, an essential part of his portrait. He sits at his writing table, now stripped of all clues to his profession except for his writing board, which Zut instructs him to hold down flat—an angle that Pearson has never used—and to pretend to write. As Zut photographs him, he continues his silent monologue.

He makes fun of his eighty-something face ("a cup of soup with handles sticking out"), as Pritchett had made fun of his seventy-year-old face in *Midnight Oil*. But in this later soliloquy on his face, he is mourning, half-comically, not only the physical changes brought about by age (he only sees those when he shaves, he says), but the increasing loss of connection between his inner and outer selves.

He begins with this challenge to Zut:

> But how do you know you've got me? My soul spreads all over my body, even in my feet. My face is nothing. At my age I don't need it. It is no more than a servant I push around before me. Or a football I kick ahead of me, taking all the blows, in shops, in the streets.... I send it to smirk

at parties, to give lectures. It has a mouth. I've no idea what it says. It calls people by the wrong names. It is an indiscriminate little grinner. It kisses people I've never met. The only time my face and I exchange a word is when I shave. Then it sulks [160].

Then the flashback is over and we are back at the opening of Zut's exhibition. Pearson comes in to look at his photograph, stays ten minutes, and leaves, screaming (silently) at Zut: "What do I see at the bottom of your picture? A high haunted room whose books topple. Not a room indeed, but a dank cistern or aquarium of stale water ... [and] the bald head of a melancholy frog, its feet clinging to a log, floating in literature..." (164).

The story ends where it began. Pearson is on the bus leaving the exhibition and (silently) telling the passengers that "a man called Zut, a photographer, an artist ... had exhibited his picture, but by a mysterious accident of art had portrayed his soul instead of mine.... A man in the image trade, like myself, Pearson called back as he got off the bus." But, unlike Pearson-Pritchett, Zut does not efface himself in order to reveal the souls of his characters. The last sentence of the story is appropriate for the self-effacing writer: "No one noticed Pearson getting off" (164).

2

Interview with V. S. Pritchett

The interview took place on July 30, 1990, in Pritchett's home in London, one of a row of tall, narrow terrace houses on the edge of Regent's Park, where Sir Victor and Lady Pritchett—he was knighted in 1975—had lived since the early 1960s. Lady Pritchett, a handsome, vigorous woman, greeted me at the front door and directed me to the landing at the bottom of the stairs, where VSP (as his wife and everyone else called him) was waiting in front of a large window that overlooked trees and gardens—a view I recognized from "The Image Trade," Pritchett's fictional self-portrait in old age.

Short and slight, with an endearing lopsided smile, Pritchett was like the "voice" in his books: kindly, curious, quietly humorous. At almost ninety, he walked briskly up the flight of stairs to the sitting room where, with no apparent fatigue, he chatted and answered questions for over an hour. The only reminders of Pritchett's age were an intermittent chesty cough, his occasional annoyance with a no longer reliable memory for book titles, and a suggestion of sadness when he talked about his present writing routine. "I'm being rather lazy at the moment," he said, conceding reluctantly that perhaps one slowed down as one grew older. He had written for sixty years, "absolutely perpetually, seven days a week," Pritchett said, and this relief from constant labor was unwelcome.

Nor was he content to rest on his laurels. After I returned to New York I sent Pritchett an actor's reading of "The Diver," his hilarious and poignant story of a young man's sexual initiation, recorded live in front of an audibly enthusiastic audience. Pritchett responded with a gracious letter in which he thanked me for "adding glitter" to his (ninetieth) birthday. Dorothy Pritchett wrote to me separately, and tellingly, that "the story, written to be read aloud, doesn't have a false word in it when spoken, so it gives me great ammunition in my desire to make Victor satisfied and indeed delighted with what he's done."

Esther Harriott: *You've written in almost every literary form. Do you have a special affection for any particular genre?*

V. S. Pritchett: I prefer the short story, though I've always been very much engaged with travel writing, because that's really how I learned to write at all. I left school on my sixteenth birthday and was sent to work as a messenger in a leather warehouse. I stuck it out for four years, and then, when I was twenty, the first World War ended and I thought, "At last I'm free of all this. Now I can do what I really want to do," which was to educate myself by going abroad. So I went to France where I worked in the glue and shellac trade and began to write sketches. I was rather good at languages—I am awfully annoyed that I don't know Russian at all, but I became extremely good at French and German and Spanish, and even Portuguese. My earnings were very, very small indeed and, as it was expensive to hire a car or to go by bus or train, I traveled on foot. Over the next few years I walked across France, Ireland, and Spain. They were my universities.

Harriott: *Your writing is active and sensuous, full of sights and sounds and smells—the writing of a traveler. So much of it seems to be based on your actual movement.*

Pritchett: I think that is true. I've got a wandering sort of disposition. I don't walk the distances that I used to, certainly, but I walk across Regent's Park several times a week, which is quite a step for a man of my age. I can easily walk ten or twelve miles—I don't go in for it every day, I may say.

Harriott: *Has your style changed as you've grown older?*

Pritchett: I think that my style must have changed. It's influenced by other writers when one is younger. When I first started, I did a tremendous amount of overwriting. I was very keen on that rather bad writer, Hilaire Belloc, who in my day had a great reputation. He liked lavish language and all sorts of images and a certain amount of showing off. That really got me for a very short time, and then I realized that this couldn't go on. But in doing this, I hit upon my own style.

2—Interview with V. S. Pritchett

How would you describe the way your style evolved through the years?

The thing is to be yourself as you happen to be at whatever age you are. What to me was extremely important was dialogue, how people speak in their ordinary life. It's mainly listening to how people talk, what they say, how they compose their sentences, things like that. I write good dialogue—I know exactly how a certain kind of person speaks and the kind of language that he's liable to use. Popular speech has a great deal of attraction for me. It changes, of course, from generation to generation. I don't suppose I write like popular speech today, because I don't know it well enough, but I write it down if I hear it. I always thought that if I could write dialogue quite simply, that would be a good test.

What about the writing that doesn't depend on dialogue—your literary criticism, for instance?

The necessary thing in criticism is to find out what the author himself is like, so that if you're talking about someone like [Samuel] Richardson, say, you go back to the eighteenth century and you see how the century formed him. You mustn't reproach him for not being able to write popular dialogue, for example. He may have preferred to write sententious dialogue simply because that is what people thought was the thing to do. It's no good complaining that a mid-eighteenth-century writer doesn't write like a mid-nineteenth-century writer. You must understand the mental or the imaginative world he lives in and the language which he is accustomed to hear. He is, in fact, describing the life that he sees.

You've said that the storyteller "unselfs" himself in order to bring the selves of others to life, and you've done that with the writers in your literary criticism as surely as you've done it with the characters in your stories. When you write, do you try to enter into the consciousness of the other person, real or imaginary?

Yes, you've got to stop being you and try being him. But the writer is trying to get at something in himself too—all writing is a form of self-discovery.

In a speech that you gave to the London Society of Authors, you said that the "self of old age" was missing from twentieth-century fiction. Why is that self not written about, do you suppose?

I think probably as you get older you utter general impressions of things, whereas what you ought to do is look at yourself and the events around you, and see them not as elderly reflections, but as activities that are going on. Most people writing about old age are simply making speeches about it. I think if people want to write about old age, they ought not write about their own but about other people's. It would be much better if I wrote about the old age of other people I know, because I see that their lives are nothing like as tedious as they probably think they are themselves.

Your humorous and moving story "The Image Trade" is about an older writer who could be you.

Yes, I found that rather interesting to write, because it was an attempt to write about aging. And in fiction, you don't feel that you are displaying yourself to other people. But in general, it's much better to write about people other than yourself.

Does writing get easier as you get older because you have more confidence and a mastery of the form, or does it get harder because your standards are higher for yourself?

I have confidence in my writing, certainly, but I must say that as I get older, I take a longer time finding the right subject.

Is that because you've written about so many subjects? You've written something like a book every other year since 1928. Do you think that maybe you just don't want to write any more?

Oh no, on the contrary, I want to write very much. I just hope some happy idea will occur to my mind from time to time. And it does. But one has to avoid generalizations in writing, so if you see a generalization coming up, you have to hit it on the head quickly and turn it into something quite different.

Your writing is based so much on observation and specific, concrete instances. Does that become a problem as you get older?

It only becomes a problem if by nature you're lazy and say: "I've thought about all of this and I don't want to think any more about it."

One must have a constantly active mind, and preserve one's powers of observation and not drift into rumination.

Is that a danger after a certain age?

A great danger, yes. Not with all people. My favorite uncle, Arthur, was a remarkable example of an old man who had absolutely passionate interests. He was very good at collecting insects, birds' eggs—illegally—and doing enormous long-distance walks, but also, at the same time, he was passionately interested in architecture. He had a total lack of education—he left school when he was twelve—but he knew every detail of the York Minster, that famous cathedral up in York. He would take me round and make the whole thing bubble with life. And he was every bit of eighty at the time. But he'd been like that about everything. He'd been like that about wildflowers or about playing games or reading. *The Anatomy of Melan*choly was his favorite book. He started reading it when he was fifteen or twenty, and he went on reading it and reading it and reading it forever. It is full of Latin and he didn't know any, so he had to get a smattering of Latin. Entirely self-educated. He was an atheist and he stood out against the whole family who believed in God. Said he'd never heard such nonsense in his life. That kind of independence of mind I admired very much. He wasn't by any means a writer of any kind, but he had the mind of someone who was very original. He certainly had an extraordinary influence on me.

Hearing about your uncle reminds me of something you wrote in an essay ten years ago when you were turning eighty—that you didn't take any credit for your continuing energy, that it was due to those "secretive gamblers we call the genes."

Yes, I was given that energy by my father and mother. Both of them lived well into their eighties. My mother had a nervous energy, my father's was more of the willful kind.

Do you think that curiosity is part of your energy too, that it fuels it?

Oh, yes, certainly. I have great curiosity—a writer *must* have curiosity. He must think there is more to find out. I am always on the lookout for the unexpected.

You've written that one's age doesn't march year by year with the calendar, that aging isn't necessarily linear—that is, subjectively it's not. Do you think that there's a sort of essential self that is ageless?

You have an initial sense of character, don't you? For instance, when you're a child you're very well aware of how different you are from your brother or your sister. You're interested in your own individuality. I had no desire to standardize myself, as it were, into a general family member. I've no doubt I am very much like other members of my family in some respects, but I clung to the differences.

And does this sense of an individual self also include a kind of interior agelessness?

I think it does in a way, but it has fewer opportunities of being vindicated. If I ceased to be able to run up and down the stairs in this house, which has too many stairs, then I should really feel rather set back.

I gather that hasn't happened.

No, not at all. I am very nimble physically. I haven't aged in that sense at all.

What is your routine these days?

My routine is to work in the morning till lunchtime. After lunch I go for a walk. I go fast asleep in the afternoon, and I start again at about four or five o'clock and go on till about seven as a rule. It varies. I used to write absolutely perpetually seven days a week, including Sunday, because I had a lot to write and it took a long time to do it properly.

But you still put in a long day.

Not so much now. I think one slows down when one gets older. Ideally, I have a long day. [*Laughing*] If I have a short one, I make it longer.

What do you mean?

I spend a lot of time on things which are rather short, to get them right.

Do you still "cry out dishonestly"—I think that was the way you once put it in an essay—for respite from your labor, when you mount the stairs to your study?

I used to feel that way very strongly. Now I'm rather eager for labor.

2—Interview with V. S. Pritchett

When I labored a lot, I used to complain. Now I complain that I'm not laboring.

What are some of the pleasures of age?

The way the affections increase. When you're younger, your feelings are very strong, very exalted. They are constantly spending themselves. You haven't so many feelings to spend when you're older, so you think more of them. They are more lasting. Another pleasure is walking. I like to walk across Regent's Park and look at the trees and the changes in the sky. If I see people I might watch them or I might think, well, they're not very interesting, let's see if there's a more interesting lot somewhere else. Walking is just a lovely way of wasting time. I can't say I've ever had "a great thought," or whatever they call it, walking across Regent's Park. But sometimes I've noticed things which have stuck in my mind. I think noticing is the great thing. The tendency in old age is not to notice, but to accept.

Is that because people become more inward-turning? Or do they think they've seen it all?

They think they've seen it all and, in fact, they *have* seen it all, or as much as they will ever see. I don't think I'll ever have a very original thought again, probably. That would be asking too much. It's enough for me to see people who are alive and just being what they are. That is interesting always. I like to see what people are up to. They're not up to very much very often, but I always find something every day which amuses me. I must say that what I really like is just listening to people, waiting for them to say a sentence which will be memorable. And you never know what that sentence will be.

3

Stanley Kunitz

In November 1995, at one of the many public celebrations of his ninetieth birthday year, Stanley Kunitz read from his collected works at the 92Y Unterberg Poetry Center in New York City. Illuminated by one spotlight on the otherwise dark stage, Kunitz stood at the lectern and, in his distinctive incantatory style, read a selection of poems that, he told us, represented significant periods in his life. When he finished, the audience in the packed hall gave him a standing ovation. Kunitz remained at the lectern for a few moments, his face serious and composed as he looked out at the applauding crowd. Then he waved and walked briskly off the stage. The young woman seated next to me was in tears and seemed embarrassed to find herself so moved. But it was impossible not to be moved, both by the power of Kunitz's poetry and by the sight of the small, magisterial figure, alone on a huge stage, unfolding a lifetime in his poems.

Many honors were bestowed on Kunitz that year, crowned by the 1995 National Book Award for *Passing Through: The Later Poems, New and Selected* (W.W. Norton). Sometimes awards given to writers late in life are for their lifetime achievement rather than for the specific late work, which may show a falling-off from an earlier peak. But *Passing Through*, a collection of poems that Kunitz wrote from his mid-sixties through his eighties, shows the poet at the height of his powers.

Kunitz's late poems were his best and his late years were his happiest. Among the rewards of old age, Kunitz said (in the interview that follows this chapter), was triumphing over the "difficulties and disasters" of his earlier years: the absence of his father, who committed suicide a few months before Kunitz was born in 1905; the shattering of his hopes for an academic career when, after graduating summa cum laude from Harvard in 1926, he was rejected as a teaching assistant at Harvard (and told later by the head of the English Department that Anglo-Saxons might resent being taught English by a Jew); his struggle to earn a living—as a reporter, as an editor of library reference books and, during the Depression years, as a subsistence farmer; two marriages that ended in divorce; years of living in rural isolation and writing in obscurity

Kunitz's first contact with the literary world came at forty, after his discharge from the army in 1946, when he was invited to teach writing at Bennington College (at the urging of faculty member Theodore Roethke, the only poet Kunitz knew). And his first literary recognition came at fifty-four, when he won the 1959 Pulitzer Prize for his third book, *Selected Poems of Stanley Kunitz 1928–1958*, published by Atlantic Monthly Press after seven publishers had rejected the manuscript. "Kunitz is certainly the most neglected good poet of the last quarter-century," the poet John Ciardi had written the previous year in the *Saturday Review*.[1] But, even after the Pulitzer, critics continued to ignore Kunitz, and his poems were not widely read.

And yet, it must be said that at that stage of Kunitz's writing career, a reader was more likely to respect the intelligence and skill of the poet than to respond to his poetry. Written in dense, multisyllabic lines and ornate language, and filled with arcane allusions, the poems were difficult, sometimes impenetrable. They seemed old-fashioned, too, out of step with contemporary poetry that was breaking away from formal prosody.

Then, in his fourth book of poems, *The Testing-Tree*, published in 1971 when he was sixty-six, Kunitz introduced a radical change in style. He stripped down the long, packed lines, wrote in direct, contemporary speech, and added humor. He simplified his art; but it was the simplicity achieved by a master, a distillation of his poems to their essence. In *The Testing-Tree* and his four subsequent collections, Kunitz produced a body of powerful lyrical poetry and evolved from a talented poet to a great one.

On Growing Old

Love Poems

The usual scenario of Kunitz's love poems was a direct address, filled with yearning, to an absent lover; but the execution of that scenario changed radically in his later love poems. Paradoxically, the late love poems were more erotic than the early ones, which were weighed down by highly wrought language and elaborate symbolism and by a declamatory tone that sounded overheated and self-dramatizing. An example of his early style is in this excerpt from "Postscript," a love poem in his first book, *Intellectual Things*, published when Kunitz was twenty-five:

> O darling, a man can cry out to his love
> All night and day, and still be comfortless.
> The meaning of a mouth, a breast, is plain,
> But what you mean to me is dipped in blood
> And tangled like the bright threads of a dream.[2]

Forty years later, the love poems "After the Last Dynasty" and "Indian Summer at Land's End," published in his breakthrough volume, *The Testing-Tree*, were also addressed to absent lovers, but the cries of anguish and fevered declarations of the early love poems were gone. "After the Last Dynasty," although addressed to a lover who has betrayed him, opens on a playful note:

> Reading in Li Po
> How "the peach blossom follows the water"
> I keep thinking of you
> Because you were so much like
> Chairman Mao[3]

"Loving you was a kind / of Chinese guerrilla war," the poet continues, comparing his former lover to Mao's army, which also kept its lines fluid and its baggage light in order to facilitate quick exits. In a more somber tone, he reflects that "even with your small bad heart / you made a dance of departures" and that "the character of the enemy" was "to fight us not / with his strength / but with his weakness, / to kill us/ not with his health/ but with his sickness."

Unlike the early fraught love poems, this one is lightened by touches of humor. The poet is hurt, not bereft. And the tone is bittersweet, even tender, in his imaginary note to his former lover that closes the poem:

> Pet, spitfire, blue-eyed pony,
> here is a new note
> I want to pin on your door,
> though I am ten years late
> and you are nowhere:
> Tell me ...
> why did you keep me waiting?

3—Stanley Kunitz

The absent lover addressed in "Indian Summer at Land's End" is Kunitz's wife, the painter Elise Asher, to whom he was married for forty years (it was the third marriage for both) until her death in 2004. The poem is set in Cape Cod, where they lived in their house in Provincetown every summer, and the poet has stayed on through Indian summer after his wife has returned to their apartment in New York. The older poet does not declare his longing, but it is felt in the sensuous language and the quiet eroticism of passages like this one, in which he describes his dream:

> Last night I reached for you and shaped you there
> lying beside me as we drifted past
> the farthest seamarks and the watchdog bells,
> and round Long Point throbbing its frosty light,
> until we streamed into the open sea.
> What did I know of voyaging till now?[4]

"Route Six" reflects a love that, if less idyllic, has been deepened by marriage. Set in their New York apartment, the poem is triggered by a quarrel, for which the husband-poet offers a charming solution:

> Let's jump into the car, honey,
> and head straight for the Cape,
> where the cock on our housetop crows
> that the weather's fair,
> and my garden waits for me
> to coax it into bloom.[5]

Spoken or thought by the poet-husband during their drive from New York to Provincetown, the poem is a funny, wise soliloquy on married love. Within its compressed form, it covers a wide range of moods and subjects. First, the husband muses on their marital quarrels, fired by "those passions left / that flare past understanding, / like bundles of dead letters / out of our previous lives" (105). Then he lightens the mood by proposing that they stow those passions "in the rear / along with ziggurats of luggage / and Celia, our transcendental cat."

When he asks his wife to keep him awake during the all-night drive "by singing / in your bravura Chicago style / Ruth Etting's smoky song, / 'Love Me or Leave Me'/ belting out the changes," he is also giving an affectionate thumbnail sketch of the wife who delights him (105–6). And in his description of Celia the cat, as she "gyrates upward / like a performing seal, / her glistening nostrils aquiver / to sniff the brine-spiked air," he conveys his own elation as they come to the "last stretch toward home!"

Kunitz wrote "Touch Me," his last love poem to his wife—and his last poem—in his ninetieth year. The first line of the poem, "Summer is late, my heart," are words that came to him, he says, "some forty years ago / when I was wild with love."[6] They are the words with which he began the last stanza of his poem "As Flowers Are," published forty years before. But in the earlier poem, the words are part of a longer line and are followed by phrases written in the intricate, symbol-ridden language that characterized his early style:

> Summer is late, my heart: the dusty fiddler
> Hunches under the stone; these pummelings
> Of scent are more than masquerade....[7]

In "Touch Me," the lines are half the length and written in simple language; what remains is a core of intensity, undiluted by linguistic flourishes. And the words "Summer is late, my heart" are followed by the poet's moving realization that now, forty years later and an old man, "it is my heart that's late / it is my song that's flown."

It is mating season for the crickets in his garden, "trilling / underfoot as if about / to burst from their crusty shells." And yet, the aged poet identifies with them: for him, too, "the longing for the dance / stirs in the buried life." He kneels down beside the crickets and marvels "to hear so clear / and brave a music pour / from such a small machine." "What makes the engine go?" he asks, and answers, "Desire, desire, desire." The sound of that repeated word is like a cry.

The poet addresses the three last lines to his wife, his passionate voice undiminished by time:

> Darling, do you remember
> the man you married? Touch me,
> remind me who I am.

The Search for the Father

The mysterious absence of his father, who committed suicide a few months before Kunitz was born—a mystery compounded by his mother's refusal to speak of him—haunted Kunitz's childhood and became a pervasive theme in his poems. Most are direct addresses to his father by the son who longs for an answer that never comes. The first on this theme, "For the Word Is Flesh," is written in the lofty diction and rhetorical style that characterized Kunitz's early poetry, which turns the son's personal appeal to his father into a formal, and rather distant, invocation:

> O ruined father, long sweetly rotten
> Under the dial, the time-dissolving urn
> Beware a second perishing, forgotten....[8]

He fears that his father will be forgotten because he has left no legacy of words or deeds by which the son can commemorate his memory. But the poignancy of this notion is undercut by the archaic language and stilted manner in which he expresses it.

Beginning with *The Testing-Tree*, Kunitz located the poems about his father in the specific milieus of his childhood, which gave them an immediacy that was missing in the vague, stylized settings of his earlier poems. "The Portrait," set in Kunitz's childhood home, is a searing account of the day that he discovered the portrait of a stranger—his father—in a trunk in the attic. The poem, which is as much about his mother's furious attempt to eradicate his father's memory as it is about his father's death, begins with this spare, ironic passage:

> My mother never forgave my father
> for killing himself,
> especially at such an awkward time
> and in a public park,
> that spring
> when I was waiting to be born.
> She locked his name
> in her deepest cabinet
> and would not let him out,
> though I could hear him thumping.[9]

The boy brought the portrait down from the attic and the poet relates, and relives, his mother's reaction. She "ripped it into shreds / without a single word / and slapped me hard." "In my sixty-fourth year," Kunitz writes in the closing lines, "I can feel my cheek / still burning."

Those lines, shattering in their simplicity, contain both the child's pain and the aging man's enduring memory of it.

"Quinnapoxet," another poem set in Kunitz's childhood territory, takes its name from the village just outside his hometown of Worcester, Mass., where he spent his summers as a boarder on the Buteau family farm. It opens in a classic boys'-book setting: a summer's day, and a boy—Kunitz's younger self—fishing in an abandoned reservoir. But the bucolic mood is soon broken by ominous signs: the fish on the boy's line gashes his thumb "with a flick of his razor fin" and he sees the sun's "terrible coals" hanging over the farm and "the treetops seething."[10]

The poem takes on a dream-like quality when his parents suddenly appear on the country road, his mother wearing her mourning bonnet and, a few steps behind her, his father in a dark suit, presumably for his burial. His mother calls out to him, but he has nothing to say to her. It is his father, "with his face averted / as if to hide a scald, / deep in his other life," to whom he longs to speak. Kunitz ends the poem with a moving and inventive image that links the boy's wounded thumb with the man's deeper wound, as he acknowledges the impossibility of communication with his father:

> I touched my forehead
> with my swollen thumb
> and splayed my fingers out
> the sign for father.
> in deaf-mute country

"Three Floors" consists of four short rhymed stanzas, which give it a ballad-like rhythm as it dances from floor to floor in Kunitz's childhood home. The poem begins early in the morning in the boy's bedroom, where his mother—or the way he feels about his mother—is evoked by "a crack of light and a grey eye peeping."[11] The second stanza goes downstairs to the living room, where "Sister," lonely for her "doughboy" (the word tells us that the time is World War I), is playing a popular song on the baby grand. In the third stanza it's up to the attic and to the "wardrobe trunk / whose lock a boy could pick," which echoes the boy's discovery of the picture of his father in "The Portrait."

In the fourth and final stanza, the boy, back in his bedroom at night, sits "bolt upright," when outside his window he sees his father flying through the storm. The poem's two images of the father suggest the boy's ambivalence: the father whom he longs to recover is also a ghost, a nightmare figure.

This ambivalence is resolved in "Halley's Comet," Kunitz's last and most moving poem about his absent father, which also exemplifies the poet's notion of "layers." "My poetry these days may look easy on the surface," Kunitz said in the interview, "but perhaps it has gained a certain … gravity as it keeps cutting through those time-layers, from childhood and youth through the eventful middle years to whatever remains for me to face, including, of course, the last brutal reality."

The poem goes back to the momentous day when Halley's Comet came to Worcester and "Miss Murphy in first grade" told the children that it was "roaring through the skies / at frightful speed / and if it wandered off its course / and smashed into the earth / there'd be no school tomorrow."[12] On its surface a simple narrative told in the voice of the five-year-old boy, the poem reverberates with the gentle ironies and poignancy implicit in the perspective of the poet in his eighties.

"At supper," the boy says, "I felt sad to think / that it was probably / the last meal I'd share / with my mother and my sisters"; but he "felt excited too / and scarcely touched my plate." His mother scolded him and sent him early to his room. When Kunitz writes, "The whole family's asleep / except for me," he is both the little boy explaining how he was able to steal up to the roof unheard and the old man who has outlived everyone in his family.

Watching for Halley's Comet to appear in the heavens, the presumed dwelling place of his dead father, and having been told by his teacher that the comet may veer off-course and crash to earth, the boy calls out in the final stanza:

> Look for me, Father, on the roof
> of the red brick building …
> I'm the boy in the white flannel gown
> sprawled on this coarse gravel bed
> searching the starry sky,
> waiting for the world to end.

The layers of past, present, and future, including the anticipation of "the last brutal reality," are in those gripping last lines when the aged poet, through his younger self, says that he is waiting for the world to end.

Layers

The concept of "layers" was a central metaphor of Kunitz's late poetry and "The Layers," a valediction to the past and a manifesto for the future, became the central poem of his old age (he included it at every poetry reading). "I have walked through many lives," the poet begins, and now it is time "to proceed on my journey."[13] But first, he must take stock of the past and, as he looks back at "the abandoned camp-sites," his "tribe ... scattered," and the friends "who fell along the way," he asks himself, using a striking oxymoron, "How shall the heart be reconciled / to its feast of losses?"

But the pain of his losses is outweighed by his determination to continue his journey to "the next chapter / in my book of transformations." He hears a voice directing him to "live in the layers, / not on the litter": rather than wallow in the past, he must use the past as another, enriching layer of his poetry and his life. The poem ends on an exultant note: "I am not done with my changes," the poet declares in the last line.

The Life Cycle

In Kunitz's late poems, love merges with death, and death with rebirth, and all are equal parts of the life cycle. These are the overlapping themes of "Passing Through," the love poem to his wife that Kunitz wrote on his seventy-ninth birthday. It is a celebratory occasion, but the poet is also aware of the approach of death, the last of his changes. "Maybe it's time for me to practice growing old," he writes in a playful tone. "The way I look / at it, I'm passing through a phase."[14]

And then he catches you short with his explanation of that phase: "gradually I'm changing to a word." It is a poignant thought, but a consoling one too: by changing to words on a page—by dying into his art—the poet will survive the death of his body. For this reader, though, the poem's closing lines are more painful than consoling:

3—Stanley Kunitz

> nothing is truly mine
> except my name. I only
> borrowed this dust.

In "The Long Boat," Kunitz contemplates death more directly than in his other poems, even though he wrote it in the third rather than his usual first person. He begins by describing the ambivalent reactions of a man whose boat has "snapped loose from its moorings" and is sailing out towards the unknown.[15] At first, "he tried … to wave to his dear ones on shore." But, as the boat carries him farther out to sea, he realizes that he is "too tired even to choose / between jumping and calling" and he is tempted by death's offer of freedom from "conscience, ambition, and all / that caring." As he lies in the boat's "cradle, … endlessly drifting," the undulating rhythm of the lines suggests a primal longing to return to the womb: "Peace! Peace! / To be rocked by the Infinite!" Only near the end of the poem does his appetite for life reassert itself, reminding him that "he loved the earth so much / he wanted to stay forever."

In his essay "From Feathers to Iron," Kunitz wrote that "the inescapable phenomenon to be faced is that we are living and dying at once."[16] He demonstrated this in a magnificent late poem, "King of the River," in which he traces the journey of a Pacific salmon from the time that he leaves the ocean, swims upriver to spawn, then fades, ages, and finally, dies. "The same geriatric process in humans takes some twenty to forty years," Kunitz pointed out in his notes to the poem.[17]

In the opening passage, the active words, short lines, and rapid tempo emphasize the young salmon's drive to reach his destination:

> nosing upstream,
> slapping, thrashing,
> tumbling
> over the rocks
> till you paint them
> with your belly's blood.[18]

Compelled by nature's insistent and seductive command, "*Come. Bathe in these waters. / Increase and die*," the salmon pushes forward, "bruised, battering toward the dam / that lips the orgiastic pool" until he reaches his ecstatic peak: "Burn with me! / The only music is time, / The only dance is love." And then it is over. Addressing the salmon, the poet tells him that he is changing "into the shape you dread / ... Fat drips from your bones. / The flutes of your gills discolor. / You have become a ship for parasites." Nothing is left "but nostalgia and desire."

But after reciting this litany of the signs of aging and decay that now afflict the salmon, the poet concludes with a description of the salmon that embodies his theme that we are living and dying at once:

> he is not broken but endures, ...
> in the state of his shining,
> forever inheriting his salt kingdom
> from which he is banished
> forever.

"King of the River" is written as an invocation, the appropriate form in which to address a great creature of the sea. Kunitz's poems about the smaller creatures of the natural world—the robins, bluejays, seagulls, field mice, crickets, caterpillars, dragonflies, hornworms, snails, chickens, squirrels, chipmunks, dogs, and cats—are more intimate in tone. He is intertwined with everything in nature, the poet says, even "that cross-grained knot / ... scored in the lintel of my door" that he has tried to seal in, "but it keeps bleeding through / into the world we share ... / Obstinate bud, / sticky with life, / mad for the rain again."[19]

He also shares the world with the pair of snakes he has heard rustling in his garden all summer, hidden from his sight until one fall day when, through a narrow slit in the shrubbery, he sees them "dangling head-down, entwined / in a brazen love-knot."[20] He puts out his hand and strokes "the fine, dry grit of their skins. / After all," the poet says,

> we are partners in this land,
> co-signers of a covenant.
> At my touch the wild
> braid of creation
> trembles.

Like "King of the River" and Kunitz's other poems about the non-human inhabitants of his world, "The Snakes of September" is an erotic poem. It demonstrates the life force that drives all of creation.

"The Round," a joyful lyric that he wrote at eighty, shows the inseparability of Kunitz the poet from Kunitz the gardener. The title is a triple pun. It refers to Kunitz's daily round of tending his garden in the morning and writing his poems at night. It also refers to the circular structure of the poem: the first line of the first stanza becomes the last line of the second stanza, as in a musical round. Above all, it illustrates the circular pattern of birth, death, and rebirth or renewal that is the condition of nature and of the creative process.

The poem and the poet's day begin in his garden. In the first stanza, in sensuous language that makes us see, and almost feel, the garden's colors and contours, Kunitz evokes the scene:

> Light splashed this morning
> on the shell-pink anemones
> swaying on their tall stems;
> down blue-spiked veronica
> light flowed in rivulets
> over the humps of the honeybees[21]

In the second stanza, it is nighttime and the poet descends to his basement study. There, no longer surrounded by light and color, he sits in the gloom, with nothing to look at but the "bloated compost heap, / steamy old stinkpile" under his window. But he picks up his notebook and reads aloud the words he has just written: "Light splashed...." [*Kunitz's ellipsis*], the poem's opening words (129). His poems germinate in the basement, just as his flowers are nourished by the compost. Decay and renewal are equal parts of creation.

The Poet in His Garden

I finally got to see Kunitz's garden in July 1996, a few days after his ninety-first birthday. My first impression was that it looked like a beautiful, blooming sculpture. Consisting of five tiers of different heights and widths, each filled with a variety of flowers, bushes, and trees, the garden extended in a long, sinuous curve from the front gate back to the grey shingle house. The five tiers or terraces had been Kunitz's solution, some thirty years earlier, to the problem of making a garden on the steep sand dunes on which the house stood; but they were also the organizing principle of his creation. Kunitz planted each tier in a different design and color scheme, but each one complemented the other four. The overall effect was an intricate, harmonious pattern.

A few years earlier, a hurricane had stripped the garden bare. All that remained were the original sand dunes. "It looked like a desert," Kunitz said afterwards. He potted as many plants as he could save and brought them into the house. When the storm was over, he replanted them outside. By the time he left to return to New York in late October, new shoots were already coming up. "The garden will grow again," he assured me. "I'm going to redo it when I go back there in the spring, and this time I'll do it just the way I want it."

Now, as I watched him clambering up and down the five tiers of his garden (like five stanzas, he said), looking like an ancient, ageless sprite, I thought of the closing lines of "The Round":

> I can scarcely wait till tomorrow
> when a new life begins for me,
> as it does each day,
> as it does each day.

Post Script

Stanley Kunitz died May 13, 2006. He was 100 years old. Six months earlier, with the collaboration of his literary assistant, Genine Lentine, Kunitz published his last book, *The Wild Braid* (W. W. Norton, 2005), a selection of his poems and reflections. The color photographs (by Marnie Crawford Samuelson) on the cover and throughout the pages of the book show the poet in his hundredth year, still working in his beloved garden. The book's title, *The Wild Braid*, is from the last lines of Kunitz's poem "The Snakes of September," quoted in this chapter.

4

Interview with Stanley Kunitz

The interview took place on May 29, 1985, in Stanley Kunitz's apartment in the Greenwich Village section of New York. I arrived at 5:30 p.m., the time that he had asked me to come. He was alone—his wife, the painter Elise Asher, was at her studio—but he performed the role of host with impressive efficiency and ease, ushering me into the living room and helping me set up my tape recorder before going into the kitchen to fix drinks. Kunitz's voice on the phone, alert but reedy, had sounded old; but seeing him in person, I found it hard to believe that this wiry, quick-moving man was just three weeks short of his eighty-fifth birthday.

The apartment occupied the second floor of a modern ten-story building, but inside, it felt like a comfortable, old-fashioned home—except for the art: The walls were hung with paintings by America's leading abstract expressionists (and Kunitz's close friends) Robert Motherwell, Mark Rothko, Philip Guston, Franz Kline, Willem de Kooning. At one end of the living room, next to a picture window that overlooked a large expanse of grass and trees, was a door to the balcony that Kunitz had converted into a winter greenhouse for his plants. (I knew from my pre-interview research that he did his serious gardening in Cape Cod, where Kunitz and his wife spent half the year in their house in Provincetown.)

Kunitz returned with our drinks and settled into the easy chair to my right. Throughout the interview he looked straight ahead into the distance as he concentrated on each question, then answered in precise, carefully composed sentences. In profile, with his prominent aquiline nose, small chin, balding head, and intent but soft gaze, Kunitz looked like a benevolent eagle.

Esther Harriott: It's interesting that you first addressed the subject of age such a long time ago in your poem "I Dreamed That I Was Old" and with these lines, "My wisdom ripe with body ruin / Found it tart recompense for what was lost / In false exchange." You regard the gains and losses of age more cheerfully now than you did then, don't you?

Stanley Kunitz: When I wrote that poem—let's see, how old was I? Maybe twenty-two—old age and its companion, death, were terrifying prospects for me. They haunted me. I'm still not wholly reconciled to the fate of the body, but I can truthfully say that I've found more rewards and compensations in my mid-eighties than I ever expected.

Harriott: What are some of those rewards and compensations?

Kunitz: Just to be rid of the hang-ups and anxieties of your youth—that in itself is a lightening of the load. And then, there's an assurance that comes out of having learned so much about yourself, why you are here, what you have done, how much is left for you to do. There is a—I wouldn't call it serenity—but a feeling of relief that you haven't completely wasted your life. Maybe you can take a little pride in having triumphed over the many difficulties and disasters that beset you. As D. H. Lawrence said, "Look! We have come through!" There's a kind of exaltation in waking up each day not out of an emptiness of accomplishment or of fulfillment, but out of a sense of having used your resources. Not as well as I might have hoped, but maybe well enough to feel that there is time still to justify the life. The persons I've known who have aged badly are the ones who don't feel justified. They can't forgive themselves for having abused or squandered their talent.

Harriott: You speak of being able to say, "Look! We've come through!" It's surprising how many of the artists I've interviewed were critically neglected until rather late in life.

Kunitz: Including me.

Harriott: Including you. Would you say that perhaps the critical neglect was a factor in your continuing productivity? That it taught you to persevere?

Kunitz: Neglect can kill. But from this vantage point, I can see that the years of my deepest discontent, when I felt I was working in the dark, unloved by the world, were the most seminal period of my creative life, a time of testing, self-questioning, self-renewal. I think there's a certain point at which you have to say that the neglect, the criticism, the rejection of one's work had some justification. To be able to admit that, to recognize my own flaws and limitations, to build on whatever strengths I had, and to overcome that sense of not being wanted is, I think, a source of reenergizing the life. Of course, you never get the attention or the approval or the honors that mean as much to you as your own sense of what you've done.

Is that one of the advantages as you grow older—that you feel a freedom from critical opinion?

Yes, you don't really give a damn what anybody says about you. You know that you have done something, or at least you hope that you have done something that will stand for you after you've gone and that you won't be ashamed of. So what does it matter if somebody doesn't like what you've done, if somebody attacks your work? Let it be. It's irrelevant, really, to your own sense of the meaning of your journey. In the end, it's really only a handful of persons whose opinion, whose taste, whose judgment you care about. It's not professional criticism, it's not academic approval—certainly not that, of all things.

I'd like to go back to your earlier remark that in your youth you were haunted by the idea of death. Was that because of your father's suicide before you were born?

That must have had a lot to do with it. The terrors of childhood were always associated with the terror of oblivion. As a child, and I'm sure this is largely because of the loss of my father before I was born, I could not even sleep at night because of the fear of losing consciousness. That was a terror that I lived with during all my early years. It really has affected my whole way of living because, to this day, I hate going to sleep and fight it off as long as I can. I practically never go to bed before three or four in the morning.

I've been trying to figure out when you sleep, because you write at night and, in the summer you garden during the day, and you're active in the two organizations you co-founded, the Fine Arts Work Center in Provincetown and Poets House in New York, and ...

Yes, but I have a long day. My writing day usually begins around nine or ten at night and then continues for as long as I can hang on.

When do you sleep then? Do you take naps?

No, I have a Puritan conscience about sleep, and napping would make me feel guilty. I don't think I've ever taken a nap in my life. So what do I do? Last night, say, I went to bed at exactly four forty-five. It then took me an hour before I could fall asleep, and I was up at eight-thirty. I suppose that may be excessive, because usually I need four or five hours. But that's enough. If I have five, I feel that I have slept out completely.

So one of your great assets is that you have an extraordinary amount of energy, compared to people of any age.

That's what my young friends say. *[Laughs]*

It's not only that you don't get that much sleep, but that ...

I'm not sleepy.

Right. Do you attribute that energy to good genes or discipline or to being so engaged with your work and with the world?

I don't think of it as a matter of discipline. My mother lived to the age of eighty-six and was wonderfully alert until her death. But I think my love for language and for the natural world is all part of the picture. And I keep going because of unfinished business. There's still work for me to do. For anyone who has a poem to write or a garden to cultivate, the days are never long enough. And I have a world of friends, mainly young people.

Is that in part because you've outlived some of your contemporaries?

I've outlived *most* of my contemporaries. But actually I feel more companionable with the young ones, especially the young poets I've worked with, including a number of former students. In many ways I feel closer to their generation than to my own.

In terms of outlook?

In terms of their awareness and concerns. I'm more conversable with them. With the old, it seems to me that I have less to say. The normal subject of conversation with another octogenarian is pretty obvious. You talk about age, and I have other things in mind.

But that wouldn't be the case, would it, if you were talking to an artist of your generation?

That's true. But even older artists, I think—not all, but some of them—have retreated into themselves, into their own image. I think that's a danger, especially if one has achieved any kind of recognition. They have become iconic figures. You cannot establish contact with their secret life. It's buried too deep inside them.

That's the penalty not only of age, but of fame, isn't it? Couldn't that also happen with a young superstar who doesn't know where the myth leaves off and the true identity begins?

If you become a superstar. Very few artists are superstars.

I was thinking of someone like Andy Warhol.

The success of his career, I've always felt, had some of the elements of a parody. It's undeniable that he created, as celebrities tend to do, a legend about himself, but in his case the legend was an artifact, assembled out of spare parts in what he ironically called his Factory. This isn't what Keats meant when he said that the poet's life is a continual allegory.

What is it an allegory of?

Of human destiny, I suppose. In a sense you incarnate the whole human process. I think that every artist—it doesn't matter what medium you work in—does have that sense of being a representative human being and one who is living most fully. Coleridge said that the poet is one who puts the whole soul of man into activity. I think of it in a somewhat different way. I have this image of a house. We occupy this house, which is our bodily frame, and for most persons maybe three or four lights in the house are burning and the rest is in darkness. But the creative imagination calls for turning all the lights on, for the house to be ablaze with light. That's what one lives for, really—those moments when you feel that blazing luminosity within.

Is there any way that those of us who are not creative artists can turn on all those lights? Is it a matter of being passionately engaged with something?

I think a lot of it has to do with the extent of one's curiosity and caring. What bothers me about so many people is how little curiosity they have about what's happening to others, what's happening in the world. To me, the day's news is terribly important. The first thing I do in the morning is read the *New York Times*. There are so many things happening that I've been so much involved in—the fight for individual liberties, the whole area of human rights, civil rights, and just the political and economic life of our society. The imagination renews itself by intermeshing with the dynamics of history.

What is your feeling when you read about the regression to old ethnic hatreds? Do you despair about progress?

It isn't a question of progress, it's a question of concern. I don't delude myself that the world is getting any better or that people are getting any better. Perhaps the state of the individual has improved at the subsistence level, but the relative quotient of good to evil in the world, has, if anything, in this century—a century that includes the Holocaust—probably deteriorated. I don't think that one cares about the world in order to feel good. It's to engage one's feelings, to have some concerns apart from the private ones, to have a sense that you are a representative human being and that what happens to others is happening to you. Even to be able to confront each day with what Ortega y Gasset called "the assaults of existence" is part of the process of staying alive.

And some of those assaults can have their own kind of exaltation?

Yes, exactly. Just to know, to be aware of them, and to fight them. And of course, the greater the terror, the greater the exaltation in being able to embrace it, to meet it, to resist it, all at once.

Did you know that Rollo May used you as an example in his book The Courage to Create? He said that you wrote your poems out of a rage against death.

As I told you, death from the very beginning was my adversary. There certainly was a period when I raged against all sorts of things. But mainly, I think, it was the idea of being mortal that offended me most. Perhaps it's still at the root of my persistence in staying alive. I want to outwit the enemy.

Could it be that the feeling that the work is yet to be finished contributes to longevity? That you must stay alive in order to finish it?

4—Interview with Stanley Kunitz

There is work to be done. It's never finished, you're never content with it. When you're not writing, when you're not creating something, you feel that you're wasting yourself, that you're not making the fullest use of whatever was given to you. I don't think that a poet is ever able to say, "I have done everything I could. Now I'm going to sit in the sun and simply loll for the rest of my life." There's always something to be said, and you discover every day something new about your responses to the life around you, even if it's only another image that communicates your sense of what it means to be alive. I think that is really the work of the poet—to tell what it means to be alive at this moment in history.

In much of your poetry you seem to hold a tragic view of life. And yet you also seem to be blessed with a sanguine temperament.

That goes back to what we were talking about. To understand and confront the terrors is exalting. If one didn't fear anything, if one had no real sense of what it means to be oblivious forever, then the life itself would be less precious. But to understand oblivion is to hold on to this precious gift, no matter how terrible, with all one's strength. I'll refer you to Aristotle's *Poetics* for an explanation of why the tragic imagination is more compatible with a sanguine temperament, as you put it, than with a melancholy one. The tragic view leads to exaltation, not to depression.

You've written that you envy your painter friends because they're not working out of their insides all the time.

They're not writing out of their gut and it's a physical activity. Poetry is spun out of one's breath and tissue. It's an extraordinarily internal affair, different from any other art, I think, with the possible exception of music.

Is writing essays a different kind of process for you?

They're hard for me to write. I spend as much care on them as I do on a poem. Sometimes it's excruciating just to get the wording right. I'm not a fluent writer.

Are you more fluent when you write poetry?

I think so, yes. Prose bothers me because I'm very impatient with the bridges, the connections. I love the fact that in a poem you can leap from pole to pole with a flick of the tongue. You trust the imagination of the reader and you trust your own imagination that the leap has a meaning in itself, that there is a connection. But, especially in expository prose, you have to maintain the flow and the sense of linkage, sentence to sentence, paragraph to paragraph.

But I think that your essays in A Kind of Order, a Kind of Folly are extraordinarily fluid.

That encourages me to proceed with my plan to put out a new and expanded collection. The old one has been out of print for some time. As it happens, I'm in the process now of negotiating contracts for three books—which shows you [*laughing*] how sanguine I am about the future.

Do you think that there has been a change in your style as you've grown older?

Everybody says so. But I also think there is a continuity, an abiding principle. I say this in the beginning of the poem called "The Layers": "I have walked through many lives, / some of them my own, / and I am not who I was, / though some principle of being abides, from which I struggle / not to stray."

There has certainly been a continuity in your themes and concerns, but what about the style itself? In your essay, also called "The Layers," you wrote, "In my later years I have wanted to write poems that are simple on the surface, even transparent in their diction."

I wanted a voice that was freer and more quickly responsive to the fluctuations of my feelings, and so I broke with the formal tradition. But that doesn't mean that I've abandoned form or structure. I simply have a more flexible pattern and a less constrictive mode of expression.

The development of your poetic style reminds me of Yeats's development. In both cases the early poems are more decorative, the later ones are simpler in form and more powerful.

Yeats was one of my early heroes and I learned a lot from him. His early poems were quite soft and misty, full of legend and folklore, not an embodiment of his inner turmoil. I have no great love for the early Yeats—the late Yeats is the one who spoke to me and still speaks to me. As he grew older, he began to speak directly of his feelings about Ireland, about Maud Gonne, and about the two matters that he felt were the only legitimate concern of an old poet, namely sex and death.

Do you agree with him on that?

It depends on the interpretation of his terms. If you stretch his pair of themes to their referential limits they cover practically everything, the sacred as well as the profane.

In your poem "Raccoon Journal," you speak of "the separate wilderness of age, / where the old, libidinous beasts / assume familiar shapes, / pretending to be tamed." I find that last phrase, "pretending to be tamed," particularly provocative. Would you care to comment?

Perhaps I'm saying, "Don't be deceived by this old man's mask of civility and resignation. There's a wilderness inside him."

Wordsworth said that poets are best in their youth.

That's when poetry is a glandular phenomenon. Your skin secretes it. Everything you touch glistens. At a later stage you have to go down into the depths for your poems, back to your origins, to the first stirrings of the self. You have to plunge as deep into your life as you possibly can, and then you have to fight your way back. The difference is substantial, and I think it explains the distinction between early and late work. A poet of my age is a many-layered creature. My poetry these days may look easy on the surface—transparent, as I like to say—but perhaps it has gained a certain elemental gravity as it keeps cutting through those time-layers, from childhood and youth through the eventful middle years to whatever remains for me to face, including, of course, the last brutal reality. That recognition saturates the text. It both taints and sweetens every word I write.

5

Doris Lessing

On October 11, 2007, eleven days before her eighty-eighth birthday, Doris Lessing learned that she had won the Nobel Prize. Because she was out shopping for groceries when the Swedish Academy called, Lessing heard the news from the reporters camped on her doorstep, waiting for her to come home. In a priceless scene that was captured by their television cameras, a taxi pulled up in front of the house, one of the reporters rushed to open the door, Lessing stepped out and, seeing the camera lights, asked if they were filming someone. "We're filming *you*!" he told her, clearly delighted to be the messenger of the good news. "Haven't you heard? You've won the Nobel prize for literature!" Lessing gave him a brief stunned look, muttered, "Oh Christ," and waved her hand in a quick, downward gesture as though swatting a fly. Then, carrying her bags of groceries and looking more like a stout English housewife than a Nobel laureate, Lessing headed for her house. (This memorable encounter can be seen on YouTube under the title of "Oh Christ.")

Over the next twenty-four hours, members of the English literary establishment weighed in with their evaluations of the winner of literature's highest prize, most of them agreeing that this recognition of Lessing's work was deserved, indeed long overdue. A typical response came from the writer Robert McCrum, who declared that the Swedish Academy had "belatedly come to its senses" in acknowledging that "the tough-minded octogenarian grandmother whom so many English readers above the age of 35 hold in such passionate regard … is one of the most important literary voices of her generation."[1]

A dissenting voice was provided by the American literary critic Harold Bloom, who accused the Swedish Academy of "pure political correctness," and went on to say that, "although at the beginning of her writing career Ms. Lessing had a few admirable qualities, I find her work for the past fifteen years quite unreadable … fourth-rate science fiction."[2]

5—Doris Lessing

While few would argue with Professor Bloom's opinion that her early work was her best, his suggestion that Lessing's writing declined as she aged left out an important factor in its evolution.

In 1969, at the age of fifty and after two decades of critical and popular acclaim for her novels, which were written in traditional, realistic style, Lessing suddenly shifted from realism to surrealism in the last section of her novel *The Four-Gated City*, plunging her protagonist—and her startled readers—into a post-apocalyptic city inhabited by the survivors of nuclear war. This was the prelude to a fifteen-year period during which she abandoned realism for non-realistic genres—allegories, fables, fantasies, "space fiction." Lessing returned to the realistic novel in 1984, but through the remaining years of her long career, she alternated between realistic and speculative fiction, and the quality of her writing varied more according to the genre of the book than the age of the writer.

This is not to say that her later realistic novels equaled her earlier ones. The obverse side of Lessing's astonishing productivity—an oeuvre of twenty-four novels, sixteen collections of short stories, six volumes of nonfiction, two volumes of autobiography, as well as three plays, a volume of poetry, and the libretti for two operas based on her "space-fiction" novels—was an increasing carelessness in the writing, as though she was fighting against time to get her all her ideas down on the page. There were few political, social, or moral issues that she failed to address, but she frequently addressed them in long passages of didactic prose.

Lessing retained her mastery of realism in her short stories, whose concise form restrained her tendency to be discursive and prolix. Without the larger canvas of the novel on which to spell out her ideas, she incorporated them into scenes of her characters' lives and the intensity of the writing was not diluted by authorial intrusions.

Always attuned to the spirit of the time—the zeitgeist, to use one of her favorite words—Lessing seemed to anticipate changes in society just before they happened, which put her in the role of a social prophet. "Lessing is the kind of writer who has followers, not just readers," observed the writer Lesley Hazelton.[3] The most striking example of this was the response of women to *The Golden Notebook*, the novel that brought Lessing to international attention and that remains her most famous book.

Published in 1962, *The Golden Notebook* was championed as a founding document of the women's movement, a characterization that Lessing rejected with increasing asperity through the years. In her introduction to the novel's fourth edition, she wrote what the book was and was *not* about (it was not, for example, "a trumpet for Women's Liberation") and complained that "some books are not read in the right way."[4] But books are not necessarily read in the way that the author intended, and it's easy to understand why *The Golden Notebook* resonated with women who were beginning to question their roles in society.

Through her autobiographical protagonist, Anna Wulf, Lessing dramatized the life of a modern, independent woman who wants to live as freely as a man, but who has inherited the traditional role of a woman in earlier, patriarchal societies. By articulating Anna's anger at the unchanging roles of women in a changing society, Lessing was one of the first writers to break the unconscious pact of silence that had concealed women's discontent with the status quo.

On Growing Old

"The consoling thing, the steadying thing, is that whether you are two-and-a-half, or twenty, or sixty-nine, the sense of yourself, who you are, is the same. The same in a small child's body, the sexual girl, or the old woman."[5] Lessing wrote this at seventy-three in her book *African Laughter*, when she described returning to Southern Rhodesia (which had become Zimbabwe) after a long absence, and felt comforted by her continuing sense of connection with her earlier self. But this comforting notion is double-edged: in old age, one's essential self can be trapped inside an alien body. In *Under My Skin*, the first volume of her autobiography, Lessing wrote about visiting her dying father, his body wasted by diabetes, and realizing that "he was inside there, unchanged ... [and] did not identify with that rotting body."[6] The disjunction between the unchanged inner self and the greatly changed body is a recurring theme in Lessing's novels about old age.

The first of these, *The Diary of Jane Somers*, published in 1983, was also Lessing's first realistic novel after fifteen years of speculative fiction, culminating in her five-volume *Canopus in Argos Archives* (1979–82). The critics complained that she was wasting her talents, and critical opinion of her work, especially the *Canopus* series, was at a low point. Perhaps this was the reason that Lessing originally published *The Diary of Jane Somers* under the pseudonym of Jane Somers.

The following year, she changed its title to *The Diary of a Good Neighbor*, wrote a companion novel, *If the Old Could...*, and published them together in one volume as *The Diaries of Jane Somers* under her own name. She began her preface to this edition with a discussion of her pseudonym, which included several digs at the critics:

> Some reviewers complained they hated my Canopus series, why didn't I write realistically, the way I used to do before: preferably *The Golden Notebook* over again? These were sent *The Diary of a Good Neighbor* but not one recognized me. Some people think it is reasonable that an avowed devotee of a writer's work should only be able to recognize it when packaged and signed; others not.[7]

The Diaries of Jane Somers

1. THE DIARY OF A GOOD NEIGHBOR

In her earlier novels Lessing had focused with microscopic scrutiny on every aspect of the lives of her protagonists. In *The Diary of a Good Neighbor* the microscope is not focused on, but wielded by, the protagonist, Jane (Janna) Somers, the middle-aged, recently widowed assistant editor of an upscale women's magazine in London, and the object of Janna's scrutiny is Maudie Fowler, her ninety-two-year-old neighbor.

Janna, Lessing's alter ego, makes the point early and often that the old are invisible to the young and the middle-aged. Before her encounter with Maudie in a local pharmacy, Janna had never seen her or any of the other old women (or the few old men) in the neighborhood. That was because she always rushed past them on the sidewalk or where they sat together on the bench at the corner. She had averted her eyes "because I was afraid of being like them."[8]

With her consciousness of this willed invisibility raised, Janna realizes that there are no pictures of old women in her magazine's forthcoming feature, "Female Images," and proposes to Joyce, the "innovative" editor, that they include at least one. But Joyce demurs; their readers wouldn't like it, she says, "it's not their age group." "How afraid we are of age: how we avert our eyes," Janna thinks, but she reminds herself that "before a few weeks ago, I did not see old people at all. My eyes were pulled towards, and I *saw* the young, the attractive, the well-dressed and handsome" (20–1).

Lessing-Janna forces herself, and the reader, to look at Maudie—at old age—and to get past her decaying body in order to discover her essential identity. She is still there "inside that old witch's appearance," Janna insists (55). Lessing creates an identity for Maudie out of the recollections of her past life, prompted by Janna and gradually revealed: her Cinderella-like role in her family, her training as a milliner's assistant, her marriage and the birth of a son, her husband's eventual abandonment of her and the subsequent removal of her son. It is a sad story, but it is told, not felt. The novel is much more powerful when Lessing focuses on the present and the physical, and shows the tyranny of the body in old age.

In an extraordinarily graphic seven-page sequence, "Maudie's Day," she follows Maudie, step by painful step, as the old woman drags herself through her daily routine. Maudie's life is dominated by basic animal needs: her day begins with a struggle to the commode in her bedroom, as she tries (and fails) to delay defecating until she has enough strength to walk down the long hallway to the bathroom:

> She sits there a long time, too tired to get up.... No lav paper, because she doesn't use it in here. She cannot find anything to use. At last she struggles to the cupboard, her bottom all wet and loathsome, finds an old petticoat, rips off a piece, uses it to clean herself, and shuts down the lid on the smell ... she refuses to let her mind acknowledge there is something wrong with her stool [114].

This passage, with its visceral language and close observation of each unlovely detail, brings to mind Lessing's description, thirty years earlier, of the mutating caterpillars on her father's farm, "fat and seething creatures rolling clumsily ... blind, silent, their heads indicated only by two small horns."[9] Like that earlier description, this one is potentially repellent, but it gives immediacy to the scene.

Lessing's style of including every detail, which made her later novels prolix, is effective in "Maudie's Day," because it makes you aware of how the formerly routine tasks—making a cup of tea, say, or lighting a fire in the grate—become overwhelming in old age. Here is Maudie as she goes through the now arduous and exhausting process of feeding her cat:

> There is a tin of cat food, half empty. She tries to turn it on to a saucer, it won't come out.... A long way off, in the sink, are her spoons and forks, she hasn't washed up for days. She winkles out the cat food with her forefinger. She lets the saucer fall from a small height on to the floor, for bending forward makes her faint.... The cat needs milk, she needs water. Slowly, slowly, Maudie gets herself to the sink, pulls out ... a dirty saucer which she has not got the energy to wash, runs water into it.... She somehow gets the saucer on to the floor, holding on to the table and nearly falling ... [115].

Maudie is too weak to take care of herself and too proud to accept the charitable services of the "Home Help" or "Good Neighbors," who are dispatched to her squalid Council flat. And she clings to that squalid flat. Her greatest fear is that she will be sent to the "Home," which seems to have taken the place of the workhouse in Victorian novels as the most dreaded destination of the poor. Lessing doesn't whitewash Maudie: she shows her "tired slovenliness" and her paranoid rages. But she also shows the frustrations that cause them, and she even as Janna admires the old woman's temper as a sign of "vitality beating there: life" (51).

To throw Maudie's day-to-day life into sharper relief, Lessing constructs a parallel "Janna's Day." Maudie has no control over her life—not even over her bladder and bowels—while Janna, fastidious and fashionable, is in control of every aspect of hers, from her executive responsibilities at the magazine to the impeccable décor of her flat. Although her day is a frenetic round from early morning to late at night, Janna doesn't have the "drudge and drag of *maintenance*" [Lessing's italics] (127). And when she feels briefly resentful of Maudie's increasing demands, Lessing fells her with a two-week siege of lumbago, with doctor's calls, visiting nurses, bedpans, et al., so that Janna (and the reader) can empathize with Maudie's helplessness and forced dependency on others.

Lessing is a storyteller with the soul of a reformer and, in her zeal to show the magnitude of problems faced by the elderly poor in late-twentieth-century London, she crams too much into the novel. In addition to her exhaustive study of Maudie, she turns her probing lens on two other old women in Maudie's building, and provides detailed accounts of the contrasting lives of sociable, independent Eliza Bates and friendless, reclusive Annie Reeves.

She also creates minor characters to represent current attitudes to old age: the Indian proprietor of the neighborhood grocery store, who comments sadly to Janna that in England they do not take care of their old, and the young electrician who, after being subjected to one of Maudie's tantrums, asks Janna, "What's the good of people that old?" What he was really saying, Janna thinks, is "Why aren't they in a Home? Get them out of the way, out of sight, where young, healthy people can't see them..." (24–5).

Maudie eventually develops stomach cancer and Janna takes her to the hospital, where additional representative characters—doctors, nurses, social workers, with their differing views about the proper care of the elderly—are added to the cast. When Janna sits in the waiting room of Maudie's ward, she becomes the voice of the author in her ruminations on age.

She weighs the advantages and disadvantages of the personal care that was given to the old by the philanthropic "Gracious Ladies" of the nineteenth century and the impersonal care given by the social-service bureaucracies of the twentieth. She meditates on death and the afterlife and on the difference between facing death at fifty (Janna's age) and at ninety. She gives a brief disquisition on euthanasia. And she makes a character sketch of each elderly patient to emphasize their individuality, to rescue them from the anonymous category of "the old."

In an uncharacteristically upbeat reflection, Janna considers the change in her own attitude: no longer does she rush past the old people sitting on the bench at the corner. Instead, she joins them, empathizes with them, admires their resilience and courage:

> I love sitting on a bench by some old person, for now I no longer fear the old, but wait for when they trust me enough to tell me their tales, so full of history. I love—all of it.... And the more because I know how very precarious it is ... they have already been felled several times, and

picked themselves up, put themselves back together, each time with more and more difficulty, and their being on the pavement with their hands full of handbag, carrier bag, walking stick, is a miracle [166].

This is as happy as it gets. *The Diary of a Good Neighbor* ends with Janna's anger after attending Maudie's funeral, arranged by the family who had shunned her when she was alive, "all of them well off, well dressed and complacent" (251). It is Lessing's anger too: the anger of a reformer at the treatment of the elderly poor in modern Western society.

As always, Lessing raises important social, moral, and political questions in the novel. What is the responsibility of the middle-aged to the old in a society of nuclear families and working wives, who can no longer assimilate their elderly relatives into extended households? How can government policies be changed to reflect these new realities? And if she doesn't offer answers to these questions and even suggests that there are none, she gives a clear-eyed picture of old age and draws attention to what was becoming a pressing social issue.

Just as in *The Golden Notebook* Lessing had suggested the problems that would confront the first generation of women to shed their traditional roles, in *The Diary of a Good Neighbor* she suggested the problems that would confront the first generation of women to face an extended old age.

"An Old Woman and Her Cat"

Before proceeding to *If the Old Could...*, the second novel in *The Diaries of Jane Somers*, it's interesting to compare *The Diary of a Good Neighbor* with Lessing's short story, "An Old Woman and Her Cat." The subject is the same: an elderly, impoverished woman who lives alone in a Council flat in London is shunned by her family and has only her cat for company. But in the sixteen pages of the story Lessing achieved what she failed to achieve in the 250 pages of the novel: instead of explaining a life, she created one.

Maudie Fowler is an embodiment of the problems of old age, rather than a memorable character. Even her cat, who has no name or distinguishing features, serves primarily to illustrate Maudie's failing strength. "An Old Woman and Her Cat," as its title suggests, is the story of two creatures and their relationship with each other, and Lessing, the author of several books about cats, writes about them with the familiarity and unsentimental affection of someone who grew up among the animals on her parents' farm.

From the opening paragraph, in which the narrator gives the salient facts of the protagonist's life, including the information that she will die at seventy, the story moves as simply and directly as a Greek tragedy to its inevitable ending:

> Her name was Hetty, and she was born with the twentieth century. She was seventy when she died of cold and malnutrition. She had been alone for a long time, since her husband had died of pneumonia in a bad winter soon after the Second World War.... Her four children were now middle-aged, with grown children. Of these descendants, one daughter sent her Christmas cards, but otherwise she did not exist for them. For they were all respectable people, with homes and good jobs and cars. And Hetty was not respectable. She had always been a bit strange, these people said when mentioning her at all.[10]

The narrator tells us that Hetty's late husband, Fred Pennefather, a building worker, was a "steady man" who always paid their bills on time, and provides clues to Hetty's present relationship with her grown children: "There was little evidence then of Hetty's future dislocation from the normal, unless it was that she very often slipped down for an hour or so to the [train] platforms.... These visits into the din, the smoke, the massed swirling people were for her a drug, like other people's drinking or gambling." Hetty was half-gypsy, and Fred had liked her for "being different from the run of women he knew and had married her because of it, but her children were fearful that her gypsy blood might show itself in worse ways than haunting railway stations" (429–30).

We learn that after Fred died, Hetty began a small trade in secondhand clothes. She "acquired a passion for moving about the streets with her old perambulator, in which she crammed whatever she was buying and selling" and for the "gossiping, the bargaining, the wheedling from householders. It was this last which ... the neighbors objected to.... It was begging. Decent people did not beg." The narrator completes the false syllogism: "She was no longer decent" (431).

Hetty finds a lost stray kitten and brings him back to her Council flat. As Tibby grows into "a large strong tom," he "ranges through the floors and elevators as though the building were a town" and his escapades turn him into "a scarred warrior with fleas, a torn ear, and a ragged look to him," But he "purred and nestled ... when Hetty grabbed him to her bosom at those times she suffered loneliness" (431).

The narrator explains that "once she had realized that her children were hoping that she would leave them alone because the old rag trader was an embarrassment to them, she accepted it, and a bitterness that always had a wild humour in it only welled up at times like Christmas." Then, in an obvious but unstated identification with her cat, Hetty would chant, "You nasty old beast, filthy old cat, nobody wants you, do they, Tibby" (431).

Ironically, it is Hetty's bond with Tibby that leads to her death, which is not caused by an illness of old age but is the consequence of Hetty's taking up a squatter's life. This begins after the Council announces that the previously ignored ruling against keeping dogs and cats in the building is to be enforced and that all remaining animals will be destroyed. And so, in the middle of the night, helped by a neighbor with a car, Hetty "left the street in which she had lived for thirty years" and moved with Tibby into a condemned house in a slum, occupied by a few indigent old women (432).

The inventory of the items that she takes with her—a bed and mattress, a chest of drawers, an old trunk, a saucepan, bundles of clothes, and the pram—is more eloquent than one of Lessing's detailed descriptions would have been in showing how marginal Hetty's life has become. But she starts trading again and "the little room was soon spread, like her last, with a rainbow of colors and textures and lace and sequins" (432).

The room was on the ground floor with a window opening onto "a derelict garden, and her cat was happy in a hunting ground that was a mile around this house where his mistress was so splendidly living" (432–3). Hetty made "a satisfying quarreling friendship" with one of the women, "a widow like herself who did not see her children either," and she and Tibby lived there for five happy years until, "in the week that she was seventy years old, came the notice that was the end of this little community. They had four weeks to find somewhere else to live" (433).

The housing authorities have offered to relocate the old women in a Council-run "Home" in the suburbs and an official comes to make the arrangements. In one sentence Lessing shows his distaste ("The young man, sitting on the very edge of the only chair in [Hetty's] crammed room ... breathed as lightly as he could ... the lavatory had been out of order for three days, and it was just the other side of a thin wall") and in one word she shows his indifference. When he sees Tibby, he says "automatically" to Hetty that she cannot take him with her (435). The next day, when the van comes to move the women to the Home, Hetty and Tibby have vanished.

"For the first time in her life [Hetty] lived like her gypsy forebears and did not go to bed in a room in a house like respectable people" (436). Every night she and Tibby slept in the doorway of a vacant house in the neighborhood until she was sure that the authorities were not coming back. Hetty knew that houses emptied for renovation stayed empty for months and she intended to live there again until the builders came.

When she moves back, this time as a concealed squatter, there is no Janna-figure to point out Hetty's desperate circumstances; but the narrator's matter-of-fact description of Hetty's necessary adjustments to her former home underscores its transition from home to hiding place and the horror of her changed living conditions:

> She smashed a back windowpane so that Tibby could move in and out without her having to unlock the front door for him.... She moved to the top back room and left it every morning early, to spend the day in the streets with her pram and her rags. At night she kept a candle glowing low down on the floor. The lavatory was ... out of order, so she used a pail on the first floor, instead, and secretly emptied it at night into the canal ... [436].

The weather turns cold and, in the unheated house with its broken window, Hetty falls ill with bronchitis. Just as she begins to recover, she sees a builder's van and two men unloading their gear and she knows that they will start work the next day. "By then, Hetty, her cat, her pram piled with clothes, and her two blankets were gone" (437).

The inventory of her possessions has been pared down to a box of matches, a candle, a saucepan, a fork and spoon, a can opener, and a rat-trap. "She had a horror of rats," the narrator says, a parenthetical comment that the reader remembers near the end of the story when Hetty dies and her frozen body, which is not discovered until two weeks later, "has been mostly chewed away by rats" (439).

Their destination is Hampstead, another area of London scheduled for renovation, where Hetty remembers seeing large empty houses, "tumbledown and dangerous ... like bombed buildings" (437). In one of these, she finds a room at the top of a flight of stairs. There is a huge hole in the middle of the floor, through which she can see down to the bottom of the house, but she examines the walls, which are "more or less sound" and she sees that the "rain and wind blowing in from the window would leave one corner dry." And in that corner, "she made another nest—her last" (441).

Again, the narrator's cool, factual account of the living conditions contrasts with, and emphasizes, their nightmarish quality. Hetty breaks floorboards to build fires for cooking the pigeons that Tibby brings in for their dinner; one morning she sees the "corpse collectors" remove the body of a homeless man who has died in the doorway of the house; and every night she hears the sound of the rats running between the walls.

Since we know that Hetty is seventy, we know that her death is imminent. Hetty knows it too. As she becomes increasingly weak and feverish from another, more severe attack of bronchitis, she reflects with an almost ironic disbelief that her death "could depend on something so arbitrary as the builders starting work on a house in January rather than in April" (432).

Lessing shows Hetty's decline into death through Tibby's changing reactions to her. Every night he "climbed under the heap of rags that was Hetty's bed" and slept "in her hard thin old arms." Then he stopped climbing in with her and instead sat "close to the old blue face that poked out." And on the last day of Hetty's life, when "she shouted at her four children that she needed a room of her own now that she was getting on, she made so much noise that Tibby bounded on to the pram and crouched, watching her" (438-9).

In the morning he left and, when he returned that night, he found Hetty "apparently asleep ... propped sitting in a corner." This is when the narrator tells us that Hetty's body was found two weeks later, "what was left of her," and we remember about the rats (442).

After a few days Tibby moved off in search of shelter for the winter, and ended up in an old churchyard where he joined a group of stray cats living there, wild. When a municipal official came to trap them, some of the cats escaped, but Tibby's conditioning in his home with Hetty was his undoing. He didn't run away from the man, who "had only to pick him up. 'You're an old soldier, aren't you? ... A real tough one, a real old tramp,' the man said" (442).

The story concludes in a brief, ironic paragraph. "Perhaps," the narrator says, "if Tibby had been younger, a home might have been found for him ... since he was amiable and wanted to be liked by the human race. But he was really too old and smelly and battered. So they gave him an injection and, as we say, 'put him to sleep'" (443).

Tibby's fate echoes Hetty's: both tough old animals are destroyed by their unspeakable living conditions and, indirectly, by the indifference of society. And because Lessing refrains from moralizing (or anthropomorphizing), the ending does not seem contrived, but inevitable.

The Diaries of Jane Somers

2. IF THE OLD COULD ...

This companion novel to *The Diary of a Good Neighbour*, set five years later, continues Janna's examination of old age; but it focuses on Janna's anguish as she faces the loss of her sexual attractiveness, precipitated by her infatuation with Richard, a married man she meets in a chance encounter that sets the novel in motion. Getting off the train on her way to work, Janna trips and is about to fall on the platform when Richard rushes over and catches her. "We took each other in, liking what we saw and showing it," Janna reports later in her diary.[11]

When she bumps into him again the next morning and he invites her to have breakfast the following day, Janna reports somewhat less casually in her diary that she "arrived at the office knowing that every gland in my body was shooting out magical substances and that my blood must be pure ichor" (267). With its references to glands and bodily juices, the language is vintage Lessing, whose responses are visceral whether she is describing a decrepit old woman or the mutating caterpillars on her father's farm or a protagonist's sexual arousal.

After their breakfast together, Janna and Richard walk through the park and Janna compares its springtime bloom to her own reawakening. "How fresh and dazzling everything was, each flower or bird an amazement, a gift of love," she exults, "and we realized a day like this might not come again ... so rare it was and how rare ... our meeting." But her elation is tempered by her intimations of mortality: "For a moment the intoxication of the day went and I saw a ... middle-aged man, ... stooped because of some invisible burden he carried ... and I saw life, the way it drags down, pulls low, weighs, tugs, erodes" (276–7).

Richard asks her for a picture of herself taken before she was married, a request that triggers Janna's emotional upheaval. She finds a picture and, comparing her "younger self (the real one)" to the "rather good-looking woman" in her mirror, "feature by feature" and "body part to body part," she concludes that "you could say, Where's the difference? But the whole ensemble—oh that's a very different thing...." The girl in the photograph is "so strong an assault on the senses, all dew and juices," while, in the mirror is "this solid woman with no light in her.... It is all achieved, done for" (285).

This scene was prefigured in Lessing's earlier novel *The Summer Before the Dark*, in which the protagonist, Kate Brown, a woman in her forties, also stood in front of a mirror and appraised her reflection. She saw that "her shape, her attributes ... were not that different from the equipment with which she had attracted a dozen young men nearly a quarter of a century ago, with which she had married her husband.... What was different was nothing tangible." It was "that emanation of ... *I am available, come and sniff and taste*" [Lessing's italics].[12]

With her choice of language in both scenes, Lessing could have been writing about pheromones, the chemical substance produced by animals as a sexual stimulus to others of the same species, which, in human terms, is presumably not present in post-menopausal women. For Kate and Janna, the loss of this "invisible substance" is the loss of a crucial part of their identities.

While it's understandable that a fifty-five-year-old woman might view the changes in her body with dismay, although Janna's reaction seems premature (especially now, almost a half-century later, when fifty is the new forty—or thirty), what is not understandable, or convincing, is the extremity of her reaction. It extends to her fear of letting Richard see her youthful picture because of the difference between what she was and what she has become. And when she finally gives the picture to him, his reaction—or Janna's report of it—is similarly disproportionate:

> [H]e stared down at that girl in her flowered dress for a long time. His breathing was shortened.... How I regretted giving it to him! How I suffered sitting there, knowing that something quite terrible had been done: by me.... [H]e sat there, looking at me, thirty years lost and gone ... he looked tired, even drained.... All kinds of thoughts presented themselves to me.... "It's unfair.... Is he blaming me for not looking at fifty as I did at twenty? ... [He's] *punishing me*" [297–8].

They continue to meet but, Janna asks herself, "How is it that two people who cannot meet without sending the temperature up ... do not make love? Is it that little picture of the young girl ... that stops me? Stops *us*?" She returns to the obsessive, painful subject of her aging body:

> Oh, I certainly have been deluding myself. Not much changed, I've been thinking vaguely, adjusting over my aging body the clever clothes I wear.... When I do think—which I prevent myself doing—about making love with Richard, woe invades me ... as if I were proposing to bring a ghost to a feast [293].

Richard finally comes to Janna's flat to spend a weekend, but they are subdued and inhibited with each other. There could be various explanations for Richard's inhibitions—for example, his feelings of guilt at the idea of being unfaithful for the first time to his wife of thirty-five years—but Janna continues to blame the picture of her younger self.

By eleven o'clock, their rendezvous is over. Richard leaves and Janna writes in her diary that "it would not have been possible for us to go into our [sic] bedroom, take our clothes off and make love. I was thinking wildly, If all the lights were switched off, what then? A thought which utterly amazed me, so foreign was it to me. And he said, just as I thought it, 'If all the lights were off, Janna—but then, who would we be making love with, I wonder?'" (310).

In the ambiguity of Richard's question, Lessing hints that he may have been thinking about something other than Janna's altered body, but she offers no explanations. Nor does she suggest why Janna is so terrified at the thought of revealing her middle-aged body to Richard, who is, after all, middle-aged himself.

The next day Janna's diary entry begins, "This morning I woke very early, grieving..." (311). And "grieving" is the underlying tone of the remaining two hundred pages of the novel, even though they are filled with activity: Janna's loving but non-sexual meetings with Richard; her visits to Annie Reeves (the old woman who was introduced in *The Diary of a Good Neighbour*), her interactions with her colleagues at the magazine; her taking in a troubled young niece, and finally—and most improbably—her farewell dinner for Richard and his wife, Sylvia, before they leave for Canada where Sylvia has been offered a research grant.

There are also Janna's encounters with Matthew, Richard's grown son, who declares his love for her, and, in a response for which Lessing has not prepared the reader, Janna thinks, "What a horror and a humiliation. That rather unpleasant young man pushed a button, set off a tripwire; at any rate, put his finger on some unknown part of me that had been programmed to hear just those words ... and ... I fell in love. I am poisoned.... I am obsessed" (461). She avoids Richard until she recovers from this "attack," which she likens to an illness (463).

The episode is brief and baffling, but this *coup de foudre* between an older woman and a much younger man is another theme that appears in Lessing's later novels. She had observed in *The Summer Before the Dark* that the "most poignant, tender, poetic, exquisite love is between an older woman and a younger man."[13] She developed that theme in her next novel, *Love, Again*, and she resolved it, happily and unconvincingly, in her late fantasy-fairy tale, *The Grandmothers*.

In the closing pages of *If the Old Could...*, Lessing is at her most pessimistic about old age and life in general. Of the helpless, incontinent, and neglected Annie Reeves, Janna reflects that "the human condition is reduced to this: we are sewers ... machines for the production of urine and shit, and the whole of human life is a conspiracy to conceal this fact." Annie is "viable so long as she can manage to deposit her wastes in the right places; when she can't, that's the end" (489).

At the end of the novel, after Janna and Richard have said their goodbyes and Richard has flown off "towards his real life, accompanied by the woman he has lived with for over a third of a century," Janna reassures herself, rather bleakly, that "into the emptiness will steal one by one, at first lackluster and inconsiderable, but then familiar and loved, all the little ... pleasures and consolations of my solitude" (502).

Love, Again

Lessing dedicated *Love, Again* to the "great cartographers of this region ... particularly Stendhal, in [*On*] *Love*..."[14] and, like Stendhal in his classic study, she set herself the task of tabulating and analyzing love in all its forms. But the real subject of the novel, which Lessing wrote when she was seventy-six—eleven years older than her protagonist, Sarah Durham—is love in old age. And the disjunction between the unchanged inner self and the changed body that Lessing had probed in *If the Old Could* ... (and before that in *The Summer Before the Dark*). reaches its apogee in *Love, Again*.

Widowed since her thirties and the mother of married children, Sarah Durham has a busy and satisfying career as a founding director of a successful fringe theater in London. The novel opens in the workroom of her flat, which is crowded with masks, posters, costume fabrics, newspaper clippings, stacks of books about the theater, and other paraphernalia that reflect her professional life. At sixty-five, Sarah is not anxious about aging and even finds herself "telling younger friends that there is nothing to getting old, quite pleasurable really" (6). Indeed, when she observes "the emotional tumults of those even a decade younger than herself ... [she] shudders at the thought of going through all that again" (8).

But by the third page Lessing has drawn our attention to the book on Sarah's desk, which lies open at a passage that is a grim reiteration of her familiar theme:

> The young do not know ... that the flesh withers around an unchanged core. The old share with each other ironies appropriate to ghosts at a feast, seen by each other but not by the guests whose antics and posturings they watch, smiling, remembering [3].

Sarah is writing a play for her theater company based on the life of Julie Vairon, a beautiful, gifted quadroon who left Martinique and moved to the South of France with her lover, a young French army officer. Abandoned by him and subsequently by her second lover, a count's son, in both cases at the insistence of their scandalized families, Julie remained in her cottage in the woods and supported herself by copying music for the master printer of the village. The printer, a middle-aged widower, wants to marry her, but after accepting the proposal that would have given her security and respectability, Julie drowned herself in a mountain pool a week before the wedding was to take place.

What distinguishes Julie Vairon from other doomed heroines of romantic tales is that she was a passionate autodidact (like her creator), who became an accomplished artist during her years of living in isolation. Before she jumped to her death, she left, in neat piles, her watercolors, musical compositions, and journals, and now, three quarters of a century later, they have been discovered, and marveled at, and have precipitated a recital, an exhibition of women artists, a television documentary, and a romantic biography. Sarah wants to write a play that will do her justice.

Julie had written in her journals that she could not "envision" marriage with the printer, but she added about his son, "I could love that one. And he certainly could love me. When we looked at each other, we knew it" (25). The comment seems almost too brief and parenthetical to mention, but it is a reminder of Janna's reaction to Richard's son in Lessing's previous novel, and will be echoed in Sarah's relationships with much younger men in this one.

Reading Julie's journals with their vivid accounts of her love affairs stirs memories in Sarah that she had "refused to admit for years because they had latent in them a dry anguish of loss." If she had not entered Julie's "territory," Sarah thinks, "she could have lived comfortably with something like a light dimming, or a fire dying down unnoticed, and arrived at being really old, hardly feeling the transition" (107).

Sarah's play, *Julie Vairon*, provides the framework for Lessing's study of love. The conceit is that everyone involved with the play, from the rehearsals in England to the premiere performances the following summer in the South of France, falls under the erotic spell cast by its dead heroine. Lessing uses their various forgettable liaisons as examples in her study. She writes in more detail about Stephen Ellington-Smith, a wealthy English landowner and the play's principal backer; but Stephen's function in the novel eclipses his development as a character.

Each of his relationships suggests a different form of love: he and Sarah become platonic friends, his wife is involved in a lesbian affair, and Stephen is romantically obsessed with the dead Julie. Stephen and Sarah also provide a running commentary on the subject of love, punctuating their discussions with quotations from classic novels, lines of romantic poetry, lyrics of popular love songs. But these thematic references clutter the novel and distract from its true theme, which is the grief of an aging woman as she confronts the end of her sexual life.

Under Julie's spell, Sarah enters the parallel world of the play and proceeds to mirror Julie's erotic affairs. She falls in love with Bill, the twenty-six-year-old actor who plays Julie's first lover, then with Henry, the thirty-five-year-old director who reminds her of Julie's second, more serious lover. But the reenactment of the love affairs of a woman in her twenties by a woman in her sixties strains credulity. It doesn't help that the men are hastily sketched and barely exist outside of Sarah's imagination. Perhaps Lessing expected this to be read as a fairytale, to match the play's fairytale setting in the Provençal woods and the magic spell cast by the play's heroine. But *Love, Again* is not a fairytale: it is a requiem for Sarah's youth and sexuality.

Like her earlier incarnations, Janna and Kate, Sarah appraises herself in the mirror and uses the presence of invisible substances as a metaphor for her sexual attractiveness. When her erotic self has been briefly restored by Bill's attentions, "in the glass, she saw a handsome woman ... who had about her a dewy look far from the competent asperities appropriate to her real age. This was because of the elixirs romping in her blood" (144–5).

But when she sits outside the theater, surrounded by the young, her reflections on aging are almost unbearably painful:

> The fate of us all to get old ... is one so cruel that while we spend every energy in trying to avert or postpone it, we in fact seldom allow the realization to strike home sharp and cold: ... one becomes ... a husk ... without the lustre, the shine. When I was young—and not so young—men were always falling in love with me and I took it for granted. All my years I was in a privileged class, sexually, and now ... sitting here tonight surrounded by the young ... [I] am in exactly the same situation as the innumerable people of the world who are ugly, deformed, or crippled [141].

The cycle is repeated with Henry. After they have fallen in love, Sarah sees in the mirror that "the ichors that flooded her body created behind [her] face ... a younger face ... which was that of a woman in love, and not a dry old woman" (186–7). And again, the episode ends in her anguished musings: "Henry was likely to be the last love.... He would remember an inexplicable passion for a woman in her sixties," but for her, after Henry is gone, "a black pit was waiting" (241). Their love was not consummated, not because Henry is married, but because Sarah "was afraid of his curiosity":

> For the first time in her life she would have asked to have the light off, while knowing there would be that moment ... when he would switch on the light to see the body he wanted.... But did she want that? ... She, who had been ... so confident that she had never felt a second's anxiety about what a man might see as he caressed, kissed, held ... *where was her pride*? [245–6].

This is a reprise of Janna's fear of revealing her naked body to Richard; but Sarah's fear of revealing her sixty-five-year-old naked body to the thirty-five-year old Henry is more believable, and sad. And she has acquired some of the hard-won insights of age. She is afraid of her life "ending now in old age with an ache and a hunger for love," but she also knows that within a year or less she will think of her present state as "a temporary fever." And "she *must* outlive that fever, otherwise she will head straight towards the paranoia, the rages, the bitterness of disappointed old age" (309).

The kind of love—or the longing for it—that Lessing captures best is in a brief scene near the end of the novel. It is one year later and Sarah is sitting on a bench in a London park, watching a mother and her two children. The mother is showering her baby son with kisses and endearments, while ignoring her little daughter or snapping at her in a voice filled with "impatience and hatred" (349). This is Lessing's view of herself as the child whose mother gave all her love to her little brother, a theme that, directly and indirectly, haunted many of her books. And it leads to Sarah's ruminations on love with which *Love, Again* ends:

> Is the awful, crushing anguish, the longing so terrible it seems one's heart is being squeezed ... only what a baby feels when it is hungry and wants its mother? ... No, she decides, the baby is longing for something

just out of its memory; it is longing for where it came from ... just as a small girl may look up, see a sky aflame with sunset ... and find herself stretching up her arms to that lost magnificence and sobbing because she is so utterly exiled. To fall in love is to remember one is an exile [350].

And then, as though to make fun of such a romantic notion, she suggests a more "practical explanation." Returning to the metaphor of the theater, Sarah wonders, "When love brings [the old] to grief, is this one way of hustling people who are in danger of living too long off the stage?" (350).

"So who is this sexagenarian sex kitten?" inquired Michiko Kakutani in her review of *Love, Again* in the *New York Times*.[15] If other critics were less derisive, they also found the story of a sixty-five-year-old woman pursued by men decades younger unconvincing, if not downright silly. Without defending Lessing's awkward rendering of her tale, I wonder if the critics would have found it less silly if she had not reversed the traditional gender roles in her May–December couplings. Here the "December" role is given to a woman, for whom (unlike her male counterparts) physical attractiveness is considered a prerequisite for a sexual affair. This was one of the points that Lessing was making: when Sarah mourns the loss of her youth and her physical attractiveness, she is also mourning the loss of her erotic life.

But the subject itself was embarrassing. This was 1996, before novelists were writing about old age, let alone sex in old age. Almost a decade later, in "The Fruit Tree," a short story by Julian Barnes, published in 2004, the middle-aged narrator tries to understand the embarrassment he feels when he learns that his eighty-one-year-old father is having an affair. He concludes that the need to think of the old as asexual is "one of the great conspiracies of youth. Not just of youth but of middle age too, of every single year until that moment when we admit to being old."[16]

When *The Golden Notebook* was published, the critics praised Lessing for the honesty with which she had written about her protagonist's sexual life. When, in *Love, Again*, she wrote with the same honesty about the ending of her aging protagonist's sexual life, the critics didn't praise it. But that honesty is what gives this lesser novel its power.

"OLD"

"Old" is the short, straightforward title of Lessing's short, straightforward essay on what it feels like to be old, written when she was eighty-five. "The approach to old age, that Via Dolorosa, is presented to us as a long descent after the golden age of youth," she begins, and argues with the writers, including Shakespeare, who have classified life as a series of stages. "Living is not so clean cut as that," Lessing writes. All the same, "that at some point along the way certain events will take place we know, we have been warned, they never stop going on about it. Teeth, eyes, ears, skin: you'd think there could be no surprises."[17]

And indeed, she is not surprised "to look in the mirror and think: Who's that old woman?" or to see herself "in old family photographs as mother, or grandfather." Nor is she surprised by "the increasing speed with which the years slip by," another sign of aging, because "that acceleration began early" (215–6). But, Lessing writes with comic indignation, "I don't remember anyone saying, you are going to shrink. My skirts, comfortable at calf or ankle length one day, are sweeping the ground the next. What has happened?" What has happened is that she is four inches shorter. "I begin to wonder," she writes, with good humor or bravado, "what height qualifies me to be called a dwarf?" (215).

Lessing returns to her abiding theme of the unchanged self in the changed body, but not in the despairing tones of her aging protagonists. Instead, she tells us, she welcomes this "permanence" inside the "fluidity" of time as a happy discovery (as she had reported in *African Laughter*), "for the person who looks at the old face in the mirror is the same as the one who shares your earliest memories, when you were two, perhaps less: that child's core is the same as the old woman's. 'Here I still am: I haven't changed at all.'"

Her happiest discovery, writes Lessing, is that old age brings "a fresh liveliness in experiencing," which she describes in a closing passage that has none of the despair that underlies so many of her novels, but is infused with wonder and delight:

> It is as if some gauze or screen has been dissolved away from life.... You don't remember feeling like this, because, younger, habit or the press of necessity prevented [it]. Everything is remarkable, people, living, events present themselves to you with the immediacy of players in some barbarous and splendid drama that it seems we are part of. You have been given new eyes. This must be what a very small child feels, looking out at the world for the first time ... [216].

6

Interview with Doris Lessing

The interview with Doris Lessing took place on October 12, 1992, in New York City. Lessing asked me to come to her room at the Mayflower Hotel, one of the cozy little hotels facing Central Park that would soon be demolished to make room for the more grandiose structures of New York's building boom. At ten days before her seventy-fourth birthday, Lessing was still attractive—much more attractive than in the picture on her recent book jackets, which, with her grey-streaked, middle-parted hair tightly pulled back into a bun, seemed deliberately plain. (When I told her this, she said that the photograph had been chosen by her German publishers, as though that explained everything.)

Nor was she a curmudgeon, impatient with questioners, as her reputation had it. In fact, she was exceedingly cordial; the only time she showed annoyance was when I asked about her writing habits. Apparently Lessing thought that questions about writing habits were silly because, as I later discovered, she had responded the same way to the same question in her Paris Review *interview several years before.*

Lessing said that she was in New York to attend the premiere of an opera by Philip Glass, but she modestly omitted saying that the opera was based on The Marriages Between Zones Three, Four and Five, *one of the novels in her space-fiction sequence,* Canopus in Argos: Archives, *and that she had written the libretto. This was her second collaboration with the American composer. The first was Glass's opera,* The Making of the Representative for Planet 8, *based on another novel in the* Canopus *series and with the libretto by Lessing, which had been given its premiere performance at the Houston Grand Opera six years before. These collaborations were initiated by Glass, whose enthusiasm for Lessing's space fiction must have been especially gratifying to her during the period of fifteen years when she stopped writing her much-admired realistic nov-*

els, was experimenting with non-realistic genres, and the critics were deploring this unfortunate new direction in her work.

Esther Harriott: *You've written some harrowing portraits of old age. I'm thinking of Maudie in* The Diary of a Good Neighbor *and Hetty in your short story "An Old Woman and Her Cat." They have to choose between captivity—that is, being sent to a "Home"—or a desperate, marginal existence. Do you think that Maudie makes her life even worse because of her insistence on "keeping herself to herself?"*

Doris Lessing: Well, when I met the original, she was getting on to ninety and she was very isolated. But her isolation was a result, I think, of her intelligence. She was not the kind of person who would want to go off to—I don't know if you have them here—luncheon clubs for the aged. So she was indeed isolated, but she wasn't confused in her mind until the very end. She was extremely angry and unreasonable, but then I think a lot of very old people are, because they feel helpless.

Harriott: *Your going through Maudie's day in so much detail made me aware for the first time of just how physically difficult each act can be for a very old person. When the trip down the hall to the bathroom seemed just too far, she would use her pants—that kind of thing. What is the answer for very old people left on their own?*

Lessing: Why do you assume there is an answer? I think if you reach ninety and you're difficult and unreasonable and quarrelsome, that's not so terrible, is it? It's not as though she were difficult and unreasonable and quarrelsome at the age of forty-three. Very old people, in one way or another, are very difficult, most of them. And I think a lot of them are difficult because people expect them to behave unreasonably or in some inadequate way, and exaggerate it when it happens. I've seen that very often. We're all of us afraid of being very old, but I don't see, apart from keeping active, and active mentally, that there's very much one can do about it, really. It's no good expecting somebody whose character is like Maudie's, essentially a loner, to suddenly change into something else.

The two other women in the book—I knew them at the same time—were the same age, both of them getting on for ninety. One, essentially a social person, was rushing around to church outings and God only knows what, every day, all day. She was always out, she had a lot of friends, and she was an entirely affable person, managing everything, no trouble to anyone. Whereas the other woman, who was the same age, decided to give up, to put her feet up. She was a grouch and a nuisance to everybody. But my feeling about that was that they were both nearly ninety, so what were we going to do—start lecturing the one who puts her feet up? People, you see, are so afraid of old age that they're looking for solutions. I don't know what—a pill, perhaps—but there isn't necessarily any solution.

Have you noticed any changes in your routine as you've grown older?
Yes, I have much less energy—much, much less energy. There's no doubt about it. So do all people who are my age whom I compare notes with. So you don't rashly undertake things you might have rashly undertaken ten years ago. You have to husband your resources a bit.

I'm not aware of your having cut down, though. You're still writing a great deal, aren't you, and traveling?
You'll just have to take my word for it. I have very much less energy, much less. It takes me longer to do things. Not physical things—physical energy is a much easier energy to have and use. It's intellectual and emotional energy. I can still walk miles every day without it bothering me. I still have more physical energy than a lot of younger people, but where it shows is the energy for writing. There I have less. It is much harder for me to organize myself and to get going than it used to be.

It is harder to come up with ideas?
No, not ideas. I've always got too many ideas. It's the organizing of the ideas and getting down to it that takes longer. And also, energy runs out much more quickly than it used to. I wrote the four or five books in *Canopus in Argus* in ten years, and two of them are long books. I couldn't do it now. I just couldn't begin to do it. That wasn't so long ago—what was it? Twenty years ago, or something like that.

What is your writing schedule like now?
People always ask this, as if it's terribly important. I've never not been asked it. I mean, it isn't important. It's a question of what habits you've gotten into.

But do they stay the same?
No, they don't stay the same, because your circumstances change,

so your habits change. But ideally—not that it happens very often—I work in the morning from about eight until twelve, hopefully with no interruptions, but that is very seldom. You know, I run a house, and everything in my life is very busy, and the older you get, the more things you're responsible for. So, this blissful peace between eight and twelve is very, very seldom achieved, unfortunately.

You say in your new book, African Laughter, *that you've always been obsessed by time, that you're in a contest with time. Because time is even more precious as one grows older, does that change the way you do things now?*

No, but a child's idea of time is so different from an adult's. I don't know if you remember at all how very long everything takes. Well, everything speeds up, as perhaps you might be beginning to notice.

Yes indeed.

So that you've barely put away the Christmas cards before the next lot needs doing. [*Laughs*] It's quite astonishing what happens. There must be some physiological reason for this perception of time.

Are you less patient with time now, more chary of how you spend a day?

Yes, because I don't have the energy that I used to have. It's very simple. I remember—it must be twenty years ago—going on a promotion trip for the Germans, who, God bless them, are well organized, and I think I must have had interviews from eight in the morning at breakfast until about twelve at night. I could no more do that—I just couldn't do it, couldn't do a quarter of it now. There is that extraordinary energy that I did have. I don't have it now. But I don't think it's a good idea to sit around worrying about it much or weeping about it. We're very good wasting time worrying about something you can't help.

What sort of schedule do you have on this trip?

A much easier one. I'm going to the first night of Philip Glass's opera tonight. This is really why I came. Tomorrow, I'm doing various things for my publishers and I'm talking at the New York Public Library tomorrow night. Then, I'm going to Washington on Wednesday and I'm going to speak at the Smithsonian—speak and read from *African Laugh-*

ter. I've just come back from Zimbabwe two weeks ago. I went there again, just to make sure I had all my facts up to date. So there you are.

Would you say that the same things are important to you now, that you have the same concerns?

I don't think I have the same concerns. I do have the same sense of self, for what it's worth. This hasn't changed in the slightest. And it's been the same since I can remember, but I don't think my concerns are the same. The concerns of an old woman are not the same as the concerns of a young woman, are they?

You're still concerned about human rights and that started very early.

That's a romantic myth. The romantic myth goes like this: "How extraordinary that you, wise child, became aware of the dreadful situation of race in Africa!" I wasn't. I had an awareness of the fact that it wasn't a very sensible situation. But what was really wrong, of course, I had no idea until I had something to compare it with, which came much later. I think what I care about, if you analyze it, is the waste of human potential. And it's what you see all the time, everywhere; it doesn't matter where you are. It's so heartbreaking, the waste of people, people who could do so much more than they're ever given an opportunity to do or be. That is what is so terrible.

It's very strong in Britain at the moment because of the slump, which we seem to think we're going to make better by calling it a recession. But the slump is very bad, and you have millions of young people who can't use their potential. You go to Zimbabwe and everywhere you find young people who are probably going to rot because they've not been educated and used. This is what I think is so terrible, that we waste so much.

You said before that not everything has an answer. Is this one of those things that doesn't have an answer?

Well, it has a theoretical answer. [*Laughs*] It's something like: why are we so stupid as to have wars when all we know is that nothing is ever achieved by war? But we go on having them. There really is a completely different—what's the word?—vision of life between people, probably like you and me, who think it's ridiculous to have wars, and, as far as I can

6—Interview with Doris Lessing

make out, the majority of people, who don't give a damn. This is what takes a long time to understand.

Rebecca West said in an interview that we have wars because men like them.

Some men do. Not all men. But then, some women enjoy wars as well. I've seen them. You know, for a certain temperament, war is a great release.

Yes, and for all those people who are bored.

Yes. That is why, I think, partly, that wars go on. The lid comes off and everything is permissible, and people who like killing can kill and be rewarded for it, and so on. We know all this, but it's very depressing that we never seem to grasp what we have to pay for it. We live all the time in the shadow of the wars that have caused us all so much damage, but we don't like to think about that. The reason why I'm concerned about it is because I was brought up with all that. I mean, I'll never, ever be free of the First World War—it's what I was brought up with. And it's enabled me to look now at people who have been in wars, and I can see how they have been damaged by them.

Getting back to what you said about continuing to have the same sense of self, does that mean that we first become aware of being old when we are perceived by others to be old, because inside we feel exactly the same?

It means that you are physically old but your inside doesn't change in the slightest. That's what no young person understands. It seems to me that there's an absolute gulf between young and old people because the young don't know that they are going to age. Bits are going to fall off in all directions, and they will remain absolutely unchanged. This is what is so astonishing.

Do you find that a good thing, that the essential self doesn't change? That you haven't turned into a different person?

I don't think I ever expected to be a different person. Maybe that means I have a quite appallingly strong ego or something. [*Laughs*] I just took it for granted. But I do find it very interesting now that I look at young people and say, "In twenty years' time, you're going to feel exactly the same as you do now, but you're going to look different." It's no good telling them so, because they won't believe it.

Do you think that our fear of growing old will change now that people are living and remaining active so much longer than ever before?

A lot more people are dying of cancer, and there's Alzheimer's—all of these things. We're right to be afraid of it. Some people's old age is just sordid misery, and for others, not at all. It just seems to be a matter of luck, really. I have a friend whose mother was riding a bicycle at ninety-odd years old. It's just luck, isn't it, or perhaps genes.

Curiosity, too. That's what I've thought about writers and other creative artists—that their energy is fueled by curiosity and by the feeling that there's more to be done.

I don't think it makes any difference whether they're creative artists or not. I don't think it's got anything to do with it.

Well, if you're a creative artist, you have a feeling that what you're doing is important. The creative artist doesn't have what to me seems like the worst affliction of age, which is to feel that you're no longer engaged in purposeful work.

I think it depends entirely on the personality of the person. I really do. I think that if somebody feels irrelevant or useless, they're going to project this. How do we judge who is irrelevant and useless? By what criterion? That they're sitting in an office from nine to five, and doing some job that is pretty irrelevant anyway, or what? We don't know what's useful and what isn't. Who judges this?

The person himself or herself. I'm thinking of people I know who have retired and who feel they're not part of the mainstream anymore. They feel they've been put on the shelf.

Being put on the shelf is a process that happens quietly throughout your entire life one way or another. This process of physically aging means you get put on shelves from the time you're thirty onward. When you're a woman of thirty, you're no longer welcome in places where a girl of twenty is, and so on. It goes on throughout your life one way or another. You don't have to wait until you're seventy or eighty to find yourself relegated to a different niche. I don't think this is something that only happens to you when you're old.

I didn't mean segregation by age so much as the feeling of the person who's been employed and is no longer employed that he or she is not making a contribution that is valued by society.

If you're going to value yourself entirely by the actual form of work you do, then you're going to be in trouble, probably. But, you know, I think more and more people do not do this. They don't judge themselves by whether they're actually formally employed, but by all the other things they might be doing. Particularly women, of course—they're always doing other things all their lives. That's why women live much longer than men, simply because of this.

You don't think it's biological?

No, I think it's psychological. I think that women are always so much busier, are always so responsible for a lot of small things that men are not. They're always much more active, emotionally and usually intellectually. I'm not saying all of them, but as a general thing. I'm sure this is why they live longer. Most women, if they retire at age sixty-five, they've got half their responsibilities still there. Like children or grandchildren or husbands, or whatever.

Some figures that I read recently showed that men who remarry are likely to live longer, and women who remarry are not.

Yes, well, I think they probably turn into nursemaids. But we're so ready to do this, to put men here, women there, and make all these sweeping generalizations. As I sit here, I can think of men, young men, or middle-aged men, who are every bit as responsible as women ever were. Things have changed so much for this war between the sexes. I don't think that the roles are so clear-cut anymore.

You once wrote that the disease of women of our time is anger, and that the unlucky ones turned it against their men.

Well, I think it's true, and particularly you see it now with this present phase of feminism. I didn't know I had said that, but of course, it's true. Of course, once again it means that women are expecting some kind of justice, which I don't know that I believe in any longer. Like what? That things are going to be fair? No, of course they're not. Ever. Still, on the whole, I think women are luckier than men simply because they do take on so much more than men do.

That makes them luckier?

Yes, being active and responsible. It also gives them vitality. Everybody in the field agrees that people getting older should keep active and busy. This is the way to keep young. It's not a new thought that people who are active at eighty seem like seventy, and people at seventy seem like sixty—that is, if they're working hard. I know women in their seventies who have enormously active lives, one way or another. It's very hard for me to think of one who isn't active and energetic and busy, and not sitting around repining at all. Maybe that's something new that's happening.

With people living so much longer, I think that the definition of "old" has changed.

When I was in Pakistan in 1986, meeting some refugee families, old women would turn out to be forty-five—partly because they were expected to be old, and partly because they'd had too many children and inadequate medicine. But I've got a feeling that it was chiefly expectation. If people expect a woman to be a crone at forty-five, she's going to be one, you know. This is what I think has happened. People no longer expect it. Good lord! A hundred years ago, you were on the shelf at twenty-eight. Just read any of the Russian novels.

Do you think that physical attractiveness is more of an issue for women as they age than for men? Or am I generalizing again about men and women?

I don't know. I've got a feeling that it's not so different. I do notice that a man of sixty can marry a girl of twenty, whereas a woman of sixty … et cetera. The only thing is, I would say that few of these marriages are ideal. But still, I think we exaggerate all these differences between men and women. I really do.

7

Mavis Gallant

Mavis Gallant is one of the greatest short-story writers in the English language and one of the least known. Although her stories appeared regularly in *The New Yorker* for almost fifty years and her published collections have received distinguished awards and prizes, Gallant's name and work are not familiar to most readers, not even, as the English writer Hermione Lee pointed out, "moderately knowledgeable ones, the sort who'd have read stories by Eudora Welty or Alice Munro or V.S. Pritchett."[1] Lee, who admired Gallant's writing and was puzzled by her small readership, suggested that "perhaps she is the kind of writer who is admired mainly by other writers."

Variations on this theme have been expressed by many reviewers of Gallant's work, among them the Canadian novelist Michael Ondaatje ("Her reputation and readership are smaller than she deserves, though among writers she is a shared and loved and daunting secret")[2] and the American novelists Russell Banks ("Here in the United States, despite having been long ensconced at Parnassian heights, she has mostly been viewed as a 'writers' writer")[3] and Francine Prose ("The question of why Mavis Gallant is not world famous—why, rather than being celebrated as one of our era's masters of the short story, she remains relatively obscure—has long puzzled her admirers, a devoted group composed mainly of other writers").[4]

The Irish writer John McGahern suggested a different reason for the disparity between the quality of Gallant's writing and the size of her audience. In an otherwise praising review, he noted that Gallant was "a scalpel-sharp anatomizer of various forms of stupidity, and while this skillfulness can often seem just and very funny, sometimes it leaves behind an unpleasant aftertaste, as if the witty, controlled prose is functioning at the expense of her characters."[5] Gallant's voice is ironic and she can be merciless when writing about stupidity or cruelty, especially cruelty to the powerless—children and servants. But she shows the pathos as well as the flaws of her characters, and her complete understanding of them is a form of compassion.

The best rebuttal to both views of Gallant—the "writer's writer" and the "scalpel-sharp anatomizer"—was provided by the English novelist Jonathan Coe, who wrote of Gallant's *Selected Stories* (published in the United States as *Collected Stories)*: "These stories are the product of a daunting talent, and this is in some ways a daunting book. Enthusing to friends during the time I've spent with it, I've found that, in this country at least, Mavis Gallant is not well known, or widely read. Perhaps people sense a superficial froideur in her writing that puts them off, or they simply don't realize that you can be brainy and have feelings at the same time."[6]

I agree with Coe and disagree with the critics who suggest that Gallant's stories are not accessible to most readers, not even, in Hermione Lee's phrase, "moderately knowledgeable" ones. With the exception of her novella "The Pegnitz Junction," Gallant's stories are not esoteric or experimental; in fact, they are traditional, even classical in style. They are not difficult, but they are dense. Each story covers as much ground as a novel, and the compression of so much material into the short-story form requires—and rewards—a more attentive and concentrated reading than readers of contemporary fiction are used to.

Most short stories take place within a limited span of time, but Gallant's encompass entire lifetimes. They move rapidly back and forth between past and present and we see the characters at different stages of their lives. The most important events have already taken place before the story begins and are presented as recollections; but not in Wordsworthian tranquility. Gallant dramatizes them in flashbacks with a mastery that gives the immediacy of the present to memories of the past.

Preternaturally observant, she describes what she sees in minute detail, but there are no extraneous words in her stories. Each sentence, each phrase, each seemingly offhand comment serves a specific purpose. When she describes the décor of a room or the style of a dress, it is to provide information about the character who inhabits the room or wears the dress. And her ear is as sharp as her eye: the characters' speech

7—Mavis Gallant

patterns are always exactly right for their age, nationality, and social class.

This meticulous attention to speech as a clue to class, typical of Europeans but not of North Americans, may have come from the charged role of language in the social hierarchy of Montreal, where Gallant was born in 1922. English was spoken by the English-Canadians, who were at the top of the hierarchy, and French by the French-Canadians, regarded as their social inferiors by the English ruling class. Gallant captured the uneasy relations between the two groups with sensitivity and wit in "Home Truths," her superb sequence of coming-of-age stories.

But her great theme was the effect of the Second World War on the people who lived through it. Her characters—Canadians, Americans, English, Polish, Romanians, Germans, Spanish, Italians, French—are exiles, émigrés, expatriates. Some have fled their native countries as refugees; some (like Gallant herself) have left their native countries by choice; and some feel like exiles in their native countries, which have been changed, as *they* have been changed, by the war. Taken together, the stories are a chronicle of the last half of the twentieth century, the postwar years, revealed through individual lives.

On Growing Old

These four late stories are set in Paris in the last years of the twentieth century and of the characters' lives. The first two, "Forain" and "A State of Affairs," are Gallant's elegies for the Polish émigrés who came to Paris after the war and are the last of the dwindling little group that, she writes, "belonged to the last chapter in the history of mid-century emigration."

The other two stories, "Lena" and "In Plain Sight," conclude two sequences of linked stories, set (mostly) in France, under the overall headings of "Édouard, Juliette, Lena" and "Henri Grippes." The headings are also the names of their respective characters, whose lives Gallant traces over four decades, beginning during the German occupation of France. In the fourth and final story of each sequence, the characters are in their old age.

"Forain"

Most of the story takes place at the funeral of Adam Tremski, a Polish émigré writer, and in the mind of Blaise Forain, Tremski's French publisher. Forain's ruminations and observations are the lens through which we see a group picture of the aging Polish émigrés and a moving portrait of Tremski in old age. His observations of the émigrés as they arrive at Tremski's funeral suggest both their increasing frailty and their increasing loneliness in old age.

They "climbed the church steps slowly," some "helped by younger relatives, who had taken time off work" and some, having "migrated to apartments in the outer suburbs, to deeper loneliness but cheaper rents," had traveled "a tiring distance."[7] The particular quality of the exiles' grief is suggested in Forain's observation that "tears came easily, not only for the lost friend but for all the broken times and old, unwilling journeys" (627).

Inside the church, Forain reflects with wry bemusement on this unworldly little group, still as innocent of the practicalities of life in France as when they had arrived fifty years before:

> Some of them had spent all these years in France without social security or health insurance, either for want of means or because they had never found their feet in the right sort of employment.... Should the end turn out to be costly and prolonged, then, please, allow us to dream and float in the thickest, deepest darkness, unaware of the inconvenience and clerical work we may cause. So, Forain guessed, ran their prayers [632–3].

But if this generation of Polish émigrés is naïve and impractical, Forain has no use for the succeeding one—those born in Paris, like Tremski's stepdaughter, Halina, or the recent arrivals from Poland, who have come to Paris not, like their predecessors, to escape persecution, but to lead more exciting lives. They are crass and materialistic, with no knowledge of, or interest in, the past. (This is an important matter for Gallant, whose stories are aides-memoires against forgetting, against the self-imposed collective amnesia about the war.)

Forain remembers that Tremski had found it "remarkable the way literate people, reasonably well traveled and educated, comfortably off, could live adequate lives without wanting to know what had gone before or happened elsewhere" (630). He knew that Tremski was thinking of Halina and her husband, a French journalist, who had not read his books even after they were translated into French. Tremski had wanted Halina "to think well of him at least on one count—his life's work" (631). But she had never accepted him, not from the time that she was three years old and her mother, a beautiful Polish-Catholic émigrée, had left her Polish husband and, taking Halina with her, had gone to live with Tremski.

Halina, who ran away from them when she was eleven, regards herself and her father as "victims of a sinful adventure" and "of better stuff than Tremski, by descent and status," clearly referring to Tremski's Jewish origins. She told Forain that Tremski had "destroyed her father, ... blighted her childhood, ... enslaved her mother," and, her final accusation, which provides a comic touch at Halina's expense, "had spoken loud Polish in restaurants" (629).

Barbara died four months before Tremski, whose "astonishing will" made Halina his heir and, therefore, responsible for his funeral arrangements. She has chosen a church in a part of Paris far from Montparnasse, where Tremski had lived (but close to her flat), and where services are conducted by a sect of charismatic Christians—another posthumous slap in Tremski's face (and an opportunity for Gallant's satire). For the burial, she has found a Polish cemetery outside Paris, which, because of the wintry weather and the shortage of cars, the mourners are "excused from attending." Before the funeral Halina complained defensively to Forain that she was doing her best and that "Tremski had never said what he wanted"—words that will be echoed, with ironic resonance, at the end of the story (629).

As he sits through the church service, Forain thinks warmly of Tremski, the most distinguished and acclaimed of his "little flock" of Eastern European writers. Unlike the others, who seemed "destined for the fate of double disappearance, their manuscripts rotting unread as they themselves die off," Tremski could have moved on to a bigger publisher (634). But he had stuck to Forain. He had also stuck to his "shabby walk-up flat on the fringe of Montparnasse, a standard émigré dwelling of the 1950s: two rooms on a court, windowless kitchen, splintered floors, unheated bathroom, no elevator..." (628). After Barbara's husband died and she and Tremski were free to marry, Tremski had spoken vaguely about finding another place; but he had kept his seedy rooms.

Forain recalls his first meeting with Barbara in Tremski's flat, the two of them drinking "harsh tea out of mismatched cups," while she asked him politely about his publishing expertise. Her preposterous questions—"Did Forain have close ties with the Nobel Prize committee? How many of his authors had received important awards, gone on to international fame?"—reflect Gallant's mischievous sense of humor, but they also show Barbara's belief in Tremski's literary gifts, long before they were recognized by others (628).

Tremski's loyalty to Forain was absolute. He had refused to listen to the other writers who complained that Forain was "unreliable" about paying their full due. Forain is a flawed protagonist. On the one hand, he was committed to keeping the works of his Eastern and Central European writers in print; on the other hand, he had "next to no money" and was "in continual debt to printers and banks" (634). But he had never short-changed Tremski, thanks to Barbara's vigilance, or, as Gallant puts it, "her forefinger at the end of a column of figures, her quiet, seductive voice saying, 'Blaise, what's this?' called for a thought-out answer" (633).

Forain thinks back to his last visit to Tremski's flat, a recollection that shows Tremski's devastation after Barbara's death and that contains the seeds of Forain's ultimate betrayal of him: "Since Barbara's funeral Tremski had not bothered to shave or even put his teeth in. He sat in the room she had used, wearing a dressing gown torn at the elbows.... He clutched Forain by the sleeve and said that Halina had taken some things of his away." Her husband had helped her carry a crate of papers that contained, Tremski said, "a number of manuscripts not quite complete." He was sure that "as soon as she realized her error she would bring them back" (631–2). Forain had responded like an avenging angel:

> He would have preferred to cross the Seine on horseback, lashing at anyone who resembled Halina or her husband but he had driven to her street by taxi.... No warning, no telephone call: He walked up a curving stone staircase ... and pressed the doorbell on a continued note until someone came running. She let him in, just so far. "Adam can't be trusted to look after his own affairs," she said.... Forain had retrieved every scrap of paper.... Fired by a mixture of duty and self-interest, he was unbeatable [632].

7—Mavis Gallant

And now the funeral service was coming to an end. Instead of joining the congregation in a last prayer, Forain "chose to offer up a firmer reminder of Tremski: the final inventory of his flat" (637). It is a good choice: the final inventory of Tremski's flat is a final portrait of Tremski:

> ... the chair piled with newspapers and journals that Tremski still intended to read ... unpainted shelves containing files, some empty, some spilling foolscap not to be touched until Tremski had a chance to sort everything out. Another bookcase, this time with books. Above it, the spread of photographs of his old friends.... In front of the window, a drop-leaf table that had to be cleared for meals. The narrow couch, still spread with a blanket, where Halina had slept until she ran away.... On the wall, a charcoal drawing of Tremski—by an amateur artist, probably—dated June 1945. It was a face that had come through; only just [637–8].

At first, the general mess and disarray suggest that Tremski was a head-in-the-clouds intellectual, oblivious to his surroundings; but a closer examination of the "inventory" reveals a deeper, more troubling aspect of his portrait. The unpainted shelves, the unorganized files, the drop-leaf table that does double duty as a desk and a dining-room table are the makeshift furnishings of someone who has not yet moved in. The only pictures are photographs of Tremski's old friends in Poland—neither supplanted nor augmented by pictures of friends in Paris, not even of his wife—and a charcoal drawing of his face, "a face that had come through; only just." It was dated June 1945, the year that the war ended in Europe. Perhaps Tremski, a Jew, was liberated then from a concentration camp; perhaps the "amateur artist" was a fellow-survivor.

The portrait revealed by Tremski's "inventory" is of a man who left the country that persecuted him, but had never assimilated into the country to which he fled. Unlike Forain's other émigré writers, Tremski achieved literary recognition in Paris; but, like them, he remained, in Gallant's phrase, "displaced and dispossessed" (628).

"Forain" is also a satire of the literary marketplace in France after the destruction of the Berlin Wall and a picture of Paris at a particular moment in history. These aspects of the story are not included in this discussion, which is limited to the theme of old age. But the brief closing scene, set in Forain's publishing house (and, like the rest of the story, inside his head), is a final farewell to Tremski and his generation of émigrés.

"More than a year later," it begins, "Lisette [Forain's longtime assistant] ... mentioned that Halina had neglected to publish in *Le Monde* the anniversary notice of Tremski's death. Did Forain want one to appear, in the name of the firm? Yes, of course. It would be wrong to say he had forgotten the apartment and everything in it, but the inventory ... filled him with impatience and a sense of useless effort. Thinking of the narrow couch where Halina had slept, Forain said to himself, What a pair those two were. The girl was right to run away" (640).

Then he "placed his hand over his mouth" and "bowed his head, like Tremski at Barbara's funeral, promising himself he would keep in mind things as they were, not as they seemed to him now" (640-1). But Forain's promise is as hollow as his pious gesture. Tremski's papers that Forain rescued from Halina have become Tremski's "posthumous novel-length manuscript ... almost ready for the printer, with a last chapter knitted up from fragments he had left trailing"—a fancy phrase for the fabricated ending tacked on by Forain (641).

Lisette, who is about to retire, has agreed to stay until she has trained her replacement, "a thin, pretty girl, part of the recent, nonpolitical emigration from Poland," who "got on with Halina and ... lost no time spreading the story that Forain had been Barbara's lover." The new girl, "gifted in languages, compared the two versions of the manuscript and said that Tremski would have approved." And when Forain "showed a moment of doubt and hesitation," she reminded him that "Tremski had never known what he wanted," repeating, unknowingly (or perhaps knowingly), the words with which Halina had justified her arrangements for Tremski's funeral (641).

The scene points out the contrast between Tremski's idealistic generation of Polish émigrés and their opportunistic successors. And it shows Forain's evolution from flawed protagonist to sanctimonious crook, whose betrayal of Tremski has extended to hiring Tremski's arch enemy, Halina, and who, after a "moment of doubt," allows his unprincipled new assistant to rationalize his betrayal.

"A State of Affairs"

This is a portrait of one member of that vanishing generation, M. Wroblewski, an elderly Polish émigré who lives in Paris with his wife,

Magda. The story is like an impressionistic poem—or in visual terms, since Gallant's stories are always visual—like a collage, composed of fragments of the thoughts, memories, reflections, and silent conversations in M. Wroblewski's stream of consciousness as he goes about his daily rounds. In actual time, the story covers part of one morning, but, because it takes place inside M. Wroblewski's head, it also covers the fifty years since the end of the war and his arrival in Paris.

In "Forain," Gallant showed the decline in the quality of the generation that succeeded these Polish émigrés. In this story, we hear of the decline in the quality of life in Poland. M. Wroblewski's correspondents, "the few who are left," complain of "the rudeness and ignorance of the young, the debased spoken language, the rise in the cost of living and in crime, the lack of good books to read."[8] And, according to the letter M. Wroblewski has just received from a Jewish friend in Warsaw, a man he hasn't seen in fifty years but with whom he has kept in touch, anti-Semitism is again alive and well in Poland.

His friend has written about the death threat he received after giving a radio talk about his wartime ghetto experiences. "On that score, nothing has changed," he writes. "It is in the brain, blood, and bone. I don't mean this for you. You were always different" (642). M. Wroblewski (Gallant uses his formal salutation throughout the story, like a sign of respect) would like to send his friend a plane ticket to Paris, find him a comfortable hotel, "discreetly settle the bill" (even in his fantasies M. Wroblewski is tactful), invite him to dinner.

He conjures up a cozy scene of his friend, himself, and Magda "around the little table in the living room with the green lampshade glowing and the green curtains drawn; or at Chez Marcel, where he used to go with Magda. The owner would remember them, offer free glasses of cognac with their coffee: jovial, generous, welcoming—One Europe, One World. There, you see, M. Wroblewski would tell his friend. There are chinks of light" (643).

"Chinks of light" is one of the phrases in M. Wroblewski's lexicon of euphemisms. Another is "state of affairs," the phrase he uses to avoid such words as "problem" or "difficulty" or "catastrophe" (648). Euphemisms and fantasies are M. Wroblewski's survival tools against his own state of affairs, which includes his serious heart trouble, his wife's dementia, and his anxiety about what will happen to her after he dies. The word "dementia" is never used: it is revealed in M. Wroblewski's observations of what his wife says and does.

He tells us that this morning, when he took Magda's breakfast tray into the bedroom, he found on the floor one of the letters that she writes and that he pretends to mail. She had written her imaginary correspondent about their teaching jobs—hers in music and his in French—at the Polish high school in Paris. "Everything in the letter is true," M. Wroblewski notes, "if you imagine that today is unwinding some forty-five years ago" (644). He describes Magda's behavior, which is a description of the symptoms of dementia—loss of memory, swift mood changes, unpredictability, reversion to childlike behavior—and his attempt to keep his tone matter-of-fact, even light, intensifies the tragedy of her condition.

"Morning is the slow time," he says, "when she refuses to understand the first thing about buttons, zippers, a comb, a toothbrush" (645). Marie-Louise, the young aide sent by the city's social services five mornings a week "knows how to coax Magda out of bed and into her clothes.... At last, neatly dressed, holding hands with Marie-Louise, she will watch a program of cartoons or a cooking lesson or a hooded man sticking up an American bank." Or, "still clutching Marie-Louise, she may say, in Polish, 'Who is this woman? I don't like this woman. Tell her to go away'" (645).

These images of Magda are juxtaposed with M. Wroblewski's remembered images of Magda in the past. He thinks back to their annual Easter holidays in the South of France. Both on teachers' salaries, they traveled third class on the train and stayed in modest *pensions*; but his memories evoke the simple, deep pleasures of "a picnic lunch of bread, cheese, and fruit, eaten in deck chairs along the front; a rest; a long walk." Magda's natural elegance, and his own, are suggested in his recollection of changing for dinner into "spotless, pressed clothes—cream and ivory tones for Magda, beige or lightweight navy for him" (646).

He also thinks of another, more recent "holiday," when his doctor ordered him to take "a week's rest, preferably miles away from home" (650). After the tiring preparations—"finding someone to sleep at the flat, two other people to come in during the afternoons and on the weekend"—he took the train to Saint-Malo. But he was "alone in a wet season," and returned to Paris before the week was up (650-1).

Magda recognized him, but didn't know he had been away. "She asked if he had been disturbed by the neighbor who played Schubert on the piano all night long.... 'You must tell him to stop,' she said" (651). The neighbor who plays Schubert on the piano, like the news in her letters, is imagined by Magda but is connected to her now-forgotten past when she was an accomplished pianist.

On the mornings that Marie-Louise comes, M. Wroblewski shops for groceries, walks Hector, the dog, and stops at the Atelier, his café in Montparnasse. In the timeline of old age, he still calls the Atelier "the new place," although he has been going there for ten years, ever since it opened in the 1980s. His age is also reflected in his puzzled and uneasy responses to the recent changes in the Montparnasse neighborhood. He remembers that his friend in Warsaw is "completely alert, with an amazing memory of events, sorted out, in sequence. If he were here," M. Wroblewski thinks, he would find "a historical context for everything" (643).

"Everything" includes "the mirrored walls ... in the new building that now rises above the Coupole" across the street from the Atelier; the picture of a naked model on the Atelier's table mats; "the beggar girl with her long braid of hair and the speck of diamond on the side of her nose," who comes to his table for money "collected for the brutal and cynical men who put the children on the street" (643). As always, Gallant's descriptions locate her characters in a specific time and place. In this story they also suggest the disorienting effect of these physical and cultural changes on an old man, especially an old man who had to overcome an earlier disorientation when he arrived in Paris as an émigré fifty years before.

A memory of that time flashes through his mind: "Of course he had begged. He had entreated for enough to eat, relief from pain, a passport, employment. Shreds of episodes shrugged off, left behind, strewed the roads. Only someone pledged to grey dawns would turn back to examine them" (646). If he is sometimes haunted by these horrors from the past, M. Wroblewski, an optimist by nature and determination, refuses to dwell on them in the present.

"A State of Affairs" is written with Gallant's characteristic double vision: it is a portrait of M. Wroblewski in old age and it is also about the enduring effect of the war on the lives of the émigrés. "The entire life of every authorized immigrant is lodged inside a computer or crammed between the cardboard covers of a dossier held together with frayed cotton tape," Gallant writes (648). The war obliterated their identities as Polish citizens and new identities were created for them by the Nansen passports, special documents issued to those whom the war made stateless. "And now, the Nansen passports are being called in" (648).

The "bureau that handles those rare and special passports is closing down. Polish political refugees do not exist any longer," Gallant explains. "They have been turned into Polish citizens ... and should apply to their own embassy for suitable documents" (648). Only a few Polish refugees are still alive, all of them too old to travel, and Gallant invents several absurd scenarios that could result from this latest bureaucratic whim (649).

The story, like M. Wroblewski's existence in Paris, is riddled with his encounters with bureaucrats, which he recalls and Gallant dramatizes. There is his visit to the mayor's office to collect "'the mayor's chocolates,' his annual Christmas gift to the elderly citizens of Paris." Gallant makes a funny story out of M. Wroblewski's Chaplinesque entanglement in red tape—so funny that a reader might miss his almost offhand recollection that this was "four years ago," which dates the onset of Magda's dementia. The chocolates were issued in Magda's name, but "she was just beginning to show signs of alarm over quite simple matters," and so M. Wroblewski "went in her place" (646).

A flashback to his chilly meeting with a German government lawyer provides a contrast in mood. M. Wroblewski was a prisoner in Dachau for the last ten months of the war and, as compensation, the German government awarded him a monthly pension, enough to "cover his modest telephone bill, with a bit over" (647). His request for an increase in the amount was denied, and the callous and patronizing explanation offered by the German lawyer who handled his claim adds insult to injury:

First of all, ... he was a grown man at the time. He had completed his education. He had a profession. One can teach a foreign language anywhere in the world. All he had to do when the war ended was carry on as before. He cannot plead that the ten months were an irreparable break, with a before and an after, or even a waste of a life [647–8].

M. Wroblewski's most recent encounter with the bureaucracy was at his bank. He had received a letter signed by "a Mme. Carole Fournier, of Customers' Counseling Service," advising him that he was "among a handful of depositors—aristocrats, in their way—to whom the bank was proposing a cash credit of fifteen thousand francs" (649–50). As instructed, M. Wroblewski signed and returned the enclosed form and made an appointment to meet with Mme. Fournier.

Their meeting provides our first external view of M. Wroblewski as an old man, seen through the eyes of the much younger Mme. Fournier. Gallant satirizes his traits associated with old age—his loquacity, his allusions to long-forgotten events and people, his unfashionably formal speech—but her satire is tempered by affection. (Her portrait of M. Wroblewski refutes any notion of Gallant as a "scalpel-sharp anatomizer.")

When M. Wroblewski arrives at the bank, Mme. Fournier is looking into her computer screen and, in profile, she reminds him of Elzbieta Barszczewska, a Polish film star of the 1930s. Instantly lost in memories, M. Wroblewski recalls that "when Barszczewska died, in her white wedding shoes, at the end of a film called *The Leper*, the whole of Warsaw went into mourning. Compared to her," he declares in his thoughts, "Pola Negri was nothing" (651).

Mme. Fournier finally turns her gaze away from the screen and begins the interview by reading aloud the questions on a printed form. "Are you sixty-six or over?" she asks M. Wroblewksi, who replies, charmingly, "I am flattered to think there could be any doubt in your mind. I celebrated my sixty-sixth birthday on the day General de Gaulle died," he adds. Then, after assuring Mme. Fournier that he didn't mean that he celebrated "the death of that amazing man," he launches into a long, meandering, painfully detailed, and very funny account of the occasion.

He and his wife were at the theater, he tells Mme. Fournier, then gives her the name of the play, *Ondine,* and of the starring actress, "Isabelle Adjani … her first important part. She must have been seventeen … the toast of Paris. Lovely. A nymph. After the curtain calls, the director of the theater walked on, turned to the audience, and said the President was dead. The audience gasped. We filed out without speaking. My wife finally said, 'The poor man. And how sad, on your birthday.' I said, 'It is history.' We walked home in the rain. In those days one could walk in the street after midnight. There was no danger" (651–2).

That last matter-of-fact observation is an amusing contrast to the dramatic tone of his preceding story, but it is also typical of an aging resident, who is aware of the changes, always for the worse, that have taken place over the years. Then, in an endearing anti-climax, M. Wroblewski tells her, "I think I've made a mistake. It was not President de Gaulle after all. It was President Georges Pompidou whose death was announced in all the theaters of Paris. I am not sure about Adjani…" (652).

The scene continues with Mme. Fournier's clumsy, insensitive questions ("Could you die suddenly?") and M. Wroblewski's good-natured, humorous answers ("I hope not"). But it eventually turns into a bureaucratic obstacle course, and the comedy turns to tragedy when Mme. Fournier informs M. Wroblewski that, because of his age and heart condition, he is not eligible for the bank's offer. It is a tragedy for M. Wroblewski because, as he tries to explain, when he dies his accounts will be frozen, it will take time before his will is settled, and his wife is too ill to handle funeral arrangements or pay the people looking after her.

But if the bank would allow his own doctor, instead of the bank's doctor, to sign for the cash credit, he would take care of everything. To this plea, Mme. Fournier replies in the bureaucratic passive tense, "The letter should never have been sent to you," she says, and adds, in her own defense, "I don't send those things out" (652).

The interview is over. M. Wroblewski "adjusted his hat at a jaunty angle," Gallant writes, a phrase that suggests both his courage and his sense of style. "Everything he had on that day looked new. Nothing was frayed or faded. He never seemed to wear anything out. His nails were clipped, his hands unstained" (653). M. Wroblewski's painstaking care of his clothes and his person is not a sign of vanity. It is his way of not showing his despair to others or to himself.

As he is leaving, Mme. Fournier calls out to him, meaninglessly, "Come back and see me if you have a problem." His gently ironic answer shows the sweetness of his disposition and the hopelessness of his situation. "'My problem is my own death,' he said, smiling" (653–4).

All of this has been recollected by M. Wroblewski as he sits in the bedroom waiting for Magda to finish her tea. "The neighbor is still playing Schubert all night," she tells him. "It keeps me awake. It is sad when he stops" (654). Her reaction of sadness when the playing stops, rather than annoyance at the disturbance, is another reminder of her unrecoverable past.

The story ends with M. Wroblewski writing an imaginary letter to his friend in Warsaw, an ironic echo of Magda's letters to imaginary correspondents. His letter is a description of his day—his state of affairs—softened by euphemism and wishful thinking. "Magda is well," he begins, and he translates her hallucination about the neighbor's piano into "This morning we talked about Schubert" (654).

"I regret that your health is bad and you are unable to travel," he continues. "Otherwise you could come here and we would rent a car and drive somewhere—you, Magda, the dog, and I." He alludes to his friend's radio talk and "its effect on some low people. There are distorted minds here too," he adds, a rare admission for M. Wroblewski, who prefers to see the "chinks of light" (654).

"Please take good care of yourself," he writes. "Your letters are precious to me. We have so many memories." This reminds him of the Polish actress Elzbieta Barszczewska and, without mentioning her name, asks, "Do you remember *The Leper*, and the scene where she dies at her own wedding?" (655).

M. Wroblewski ends his letter with an apology for not having more to tell his friend, but, he says, "my life is like the purring of a cat. If I were to describe it, it would put you to sleep. I may have more to tell you tomorrow. In the meantime, I send you God's favor" (655).

Gallant has written, "Perhaps a writer is ... a child in disguise, ... improvising when it [sic] tries to make sense of adult behavior."[9] Perhaps M. Wroblewski is like that child in disguise, improvising as he tries to make sense of his life in old age.

"Lena"

Édouard, the narrator of the entire sequence "Édouard, Juliette, Lena," begins its fourth and final story with a double portrait of Magdalena, in youth and in age. Gallant creates the portrait by focusing on Magdalena's relationships with women, an original approach that shows the contrast between the young and the old Magdalena and also emphasizes the crucial role played by her émigrée status throughout her life in France:

> In her prime, by which I mean in her beauty, my first wife, Magdalena, had no use for other women.... Magdalena saw women as accessories, to be treated kindly—maids, seamstresses, manicurists—or as comic minor figures, the wives and official fiancées of her admirers. It was not in her nature to care what anyone said ... but I suspect that she was called some of the ... things she was called, such as "Central European whore" and "Jewish adventuress," by women.
>
> Now that she is nearly eighty and bedridden, she receives visits from women—the residue of an early wave of Hungarian emigration.... They have forgotten that Magdalena once seemed, perhaps, disreputable. She is a devout Catholic, and she says cultivated, moral-sounding things, sweet to the ears of half a dozen widows of generals and bereft sisters of bachelor diplomats. They crowd her bedside table with bottles of cough mixture, lemons, embroidered table napkins, jars of honey, and covered bowls of stewed plums.... They call Magdalena "Lena."[10]

The little coterie of Hungarian women would not have acknowledged the existence of the younger Magdalena, nor would she have bothered with these "comic, minor figures." But now that her world has shrunk to the dimensions of a hospital bed, her countrywomen are willing to overlook her scandalous past and Jewish origins. They show their belated acceptance of her by bringing cough medicines and stewed plums (gifts that the young Magdalena would surely have scoffed at) and by using the diminutive of her name, "Lena."

Their homely gifts and whatever "small comforts" Édouard brings on his visits are Magdalena's only luxuries now. Age has robbed her of the seductive beauty that was rewarded with the lavish life style provided by her wealthy admirers. Even during the war, whose "rigors" she "endured" in Cannes, as Édouard remarks dryly, Magdalena maintained that style—an achievement, he suspects, that resulted from her "taking a daily walk to a black-market restaurant, her legs greatly admired by famous collaborators and German officers along the way" (822).

Now she lives in "the only place that would have her," a hospital on the outskirts of Paris that is, in Gallant's evocative phrase, "the color of jails, daubed with graffiti" (822). There, Magdalena occupies a bed "in a wing reserved for elderly patients too frail to be diverted to nursing homes" (821–2). The rules, stated and unstated, reflect the staff's attitude to the old under their care:

> The old people have had it drummed into them that they are lucky to have a bed, that the waiting list for their mattress and pillow lengthens by the hour. They must not seem too capricious, or dissatisfied, or quarrelsome, or give the nurses extra trouble. If they persist in doing so, their belongings are packed and their relatives sent for. A law obliges close relatives to take them in [822].

Magdalena, who has no relatives, cannot be evicted so easily. Indeed, "her continued existence is seen by the hospital as a bit of a swindle," Édouard notes, adding in his usual ironic tone that "they accepted her in the first place only because she was expected to die quite soon, releasing the bed" (823).

To get to the hospital, Édouard must travel a considerable distance, standing, on a crowded underground train. But he never shows his card "attesting to [his] right to sit down, because of an accident suffered in wartime." He prefers to stand, because "anything to do with the Second World War, particularly its elderly survivors, arouses derision and ribaldry and even hostility in the young" (822). As he ages, Édouard feels the alienation of an exile in his native country, with the additional irony that his alienation is the result of having served his country in the war.

He observes that Magdalena's "mind is clear, but she says absurd things. For example, she claims that she never met Juliette, my second wife" (824). He reminds her that they met once, "on the first Sunday of September, 1954." This leads to one of Gallant's dramatized flashbacks, which provides a view of Magdalena at fifty, introduces the character of Juliette, and, as a technical strategy, furnishes necessary information for readers who have not read the earlier stories in the sequence and offers variation, rather than repetition, for those who have.

Édouard married Magdalena in Paris when he was twenty-two and she was thirty-six, to give her—a Hungarian émigrée and a converted Jew—the protection of his name in Nazi-occupied France. After the wedding they went their separate ways: Magdalena to friends in Cannes, Édouard to London to join the Free French, where he met Juliette. At the time of this flashback, Édouard and Juliette have been living together for ten years since the end of the war.

Juliette, who wants marriage and children, is thirty and "tired of waiting," and Édouard is afraid of losing her. Magdalena "had resisted any mention of the subject and for ten years had refused to see me," he says. The lunch "was Juliette's idea. Somewhere between raspberries-and-cream and coffee, I was supposed to ask for a divorce" (824).

Set in the countryside outside Paris and rich in visual detail, the scene is a dramatically satisfying contrast to the muted atmosphere of Magdalena's hospital room and it deepens our understanding of the three characters and their relationships. And Gallant can evoke a character or a relationship in one sentence. Édouard remembers driving to the restaurant with Magdalena beside him "in a nimbus of some scent—jasmine, or gardenia—that made me think of the opulent, profiteering side of wars" (824). The image suggests the particular quality of Magdalena's beauty—sensual, flamboyant, decadent—and Édouard's disapproval of it.

The contrast in the clothes worn by Magdalena and Juliette provides comedy, but it also tells us a good deal about the two women. Édouard recalls that Magdalena "had on a pale dress of some soft, floating stuff, and a pillbox hat tied on with a white veil, and long white gloves.... I saw her through Juliette's eyes and I thought that she must be thinking: Where does Magdalena think we're taking her? To a wedding?" Contrasted with the inappropriate sumptuousness of Magdalena's ensemble is the plainness, practicality, and lack of vanity manifested in Juliette's "dark hair pulled back tight and tied ... with a dark blue grosgrain ribbon," and her dress of "cotton seersucker [that] washed like a duster and needed next to no ironing" (824–5).

Seated in the restaurant, Magdalena performs her customary ritual of "pulling off her tight, long gloves finger by finger and turning her rings right side up. Squeezed against a great sparkler of some kind was a wedding ring" (826). The image emphasizes her old-world theatricality and hints at her determination to remain Édouard's legal wife. Juliette, whose simple clothes, quiet good manners, and sense of propriety reflect her French Protestant upper-class background, is Magdalena's perfect foil. During lunch, with great tact and referring to the subject of divorce only in the most general way, Juliette suggests politely that "Surely ... a clean parting was a way of keeping life pleasant and neat?" (827). But Magdalena gives no sign of hearing her, and Édouard, through emotional cowardice or passivity, says nothing.

"It was shortly before her removal to the hospital that Magdalena learned about Juliette's death," Édouard says, abruptly returning the story to the present. He adds the cutting remark that "one of her doddering friends may have seen the notice in the newspaper," then gives a sardonic description of Magdalena's response to the news:

> She at once resumed her place as my only spouse and widow-to-be. In fact, she had never relinquished it, but now the way back to me shone clear. The divorce, that wall of pagan darkness, had been torn down and dispersed with the concubine's ashes. She saw me delivered from an adulterous and heretical alliance. It takes a convert to think "heretical" with a straight face [827].

We are also given the first clue that the dry, ironic, inexpressive Édouard was devastated by Juliette's death, although there is some ambiguity. He describes his reaction to the "nightmare ... in the crematorium chapel," as he calls the cremation ceremony (held at Juliette's request), when he "lost consciousness and had to be carried out" (827). But was he devastated by Juliette's death or horrified by the act of cremation?

The rest of the story focuses on Magdalena's deeper decline into dementia and Édouard's ambivalent reactions to it and to her. He tells us that he had bronchitis all winter and was unable to go out, but sent stamps and stationery to Magdalena so that they could correspond. But the letters that came from her, he says, "were scrawled in the margins of newspapers, torn off crookedly," and "the message was always the same: I must not allow my wife to die in a public institution" (827).

Then he received this message from Magdalena: "On Saturday at nine-o-clock, I shall be dressed and packed, and waiting for you to come and take me away." Alarmed, Édouard's response was "weeks of wangling and soft-soaping and even some mild bribery to obtain … public funds to which she is not entitled," along with a "voluntary contribution" to keep her in the hospital. "She has not once asked where the money comes from," he says, adding with his usual irony that, "when she was young, she decided never to worry and she has kept the habit" (828).

In April, Édouard finally went to the hospital, carrying "a bottle of Krug that he had kept on ice until the last minute," a small detail that suggests the refined tastes acquired by the younger Magdalena and Édouard's continued attention to them. But "Magdalena was not in her room and the bed was clean and empty." He thought she had died and felt "shock, guilt, remorse, and relief." Then she appeared in the doorway "in dressing gown and slippers, with short white hair. She shuffled past me and lay on the bed, with her mouth open, struggling for breath" (824).

The brusque phrase "short white hair" resonates (at least for this reader) because of Édouard's previous associations of Magdalena with the color white: the pillbox hat tied on with the white veil and the long white gloves that she had worn to the lunch with Édouard and Juliette; her custom of always wearing white linen when she traveled by train to Budapest and Prague; and, especially, the scene conjured by his memory of "the old days, in her apartment with the big windows and the sweeping view across the Seine, [when] she used to wear white, and sit on a white sofa" (823). The "white" associated with the younger Magdalena's beauty and luxurious life in the past contrasts painfully with the "short white hair" of her present state.

And then Gallant abruptly changes the mournful mood, when Magdalena suddenly gasped, "Today is my birthday." She sat up, apparently recovered, and seeing the champagne, said, "This is a good birthday suprise" (825–9). Édouard recalls that when Magdalena came back to Paris after the war, she found her apartment "looted, laid waste," and that "one of the first letters to arrive in the mail was from him, telling her that he was in love with a much younger woman." Now, touched by the sight of Magdalena—and warmed by a glass of champagne—he says to her, "If it means anything at all to you … no one ever fascinated me as much as you" (829).

But Magdalena's immediate observation that "even a few months ago, this would have been my death sentence" infuriates Édouard, and he reminds her of Juliette's "life sentence": the arrival of menopause without having had the children she'd wanted. When Magdalena points out that she could have had fifteen children without being married, it infuriates him further. "Women like Juliette, people like Juliette," he shouts at the former courtesan, "don't do that sort of thing" (829).

He adds that, even if Juliette had given birth to the son she had dreamed of, he wouldn't have been able to make a will "in his favor" because of France's inheritance laws at the time. Magdalena's reply is exquisitely maddening: "Ah, Édouard, you shouldn't have worried. You know I'd have left him all that I had" (829–30).

"Twice since then she has died and come around," Édouard tells us in the closing paragraph. "There are afternoons when she can't speak and lies with her eyes shut, the lids quivering. I hold her hand, and feel the wedding ring. Like the staunch little widows, I call her 'Lena' and she turns her head and opens her eyes." When that happens, Édouard looks away. "I have put up with everything," he says, "but I intend to refuse her last imposition, the encounter with her blue, enduring look of pure love" (830).

Gallant succeeds in making us care for this feckless, narcissistic creature, whose refusal to divorce Édouard was an act of cruelty to Juliette. Magdalena lost all her possessions without a word of complaint or self-pity, but she clung fiercely to her wedding ring, a gift more precious than any of the treasures bestowed by her wealthy admirers. Although her marriage to Édouard was in name only, she remained as devoted—and possessive—as an old-fashioned, lawfully wedded wife. And Édouard's tie to Magdalena, however ambivalent, also endured. When she grew old and lost her beauty and her senses, he didn't desert her, but remained, in his way, a loyal husband.

"In Plain Sight"

In none of Gallant's stories is the movement between past and present and from one scene to another more rapid than in this final story of her "Henri Grippes" sequence, which follows the adventures of the

French man of letters over more than forty years. At the same time, the structure of the story is as formal as a musical composition, whose opening and closing motif is the sound of the air-raid siren that "on the first Wednesday of every month, sharp at noon, wails across Paris...."[11] No one knows the reason for the siren but it sets an appropriate framework for the story, which, although set in Paris in the 1990s, is filled with images of the Second World War that constantly appear in the minds of the older residents, like Grippes, who lived through it.

As it happens, Grippes seldom hears the siren because he is usually asleep in his apartment in Montparnasse. The aging writer retains the habits of his youth, "going to bed at dawn and getting up at around three in the afternoon ... reading and writing after dark, listening to the radio or watching an American rerun on a late channel, eating salted hard-boiled eggs, drinking Badoit or vodka or champagne (to wash the egg down) or black coffee so thickly sweetened that it can act as a sedative" (868).

Grippes is glad to have reached the age "when no one is likely to barge in at all hours announcing that salt is lethal and sugar poison.... Never again will he be asked to hand over the key to his apartment, as a safety measure, or receive an offer to sleep in the little room off the kitchen and never get in the way" (868). He is referring to "Mme. Parfaire ('Marthe')," a widow and his upstairs neighbor, who, a few years ago, had suggested that her "constant presence would add six years to his life.... Now when Mme. Parfaire (no longer 'Marthe') meets Grippes in the aisle of the ... supermarket ... she stares at his hairline..." and does not speak (869).

"What went wrong?" Grippes asks himself. First of all, he "didn't want the six extra years." And Mme. Parfaire had handed him her "final statement of terms at the worst point of the day, five past three in the afternoon—a time for breakfast and gradual wakening" (869). He recalls her terms:

> Whenever he wanted to be by himself, she would go out and sit on a bench at the Montparnasse-Stanislas bus stop. For company, she would bring along one of his early novels, the kind critics kept begging him to reread and learn from. At home she would put him on a memory-preserving, mental stimulation regime, with plenty of vegetable protein;

she would get Dr. Planche to tell her the true state of Grippe's hearing (would he be stone deaf very soon?) and to report on the vital irrigation of Grippes's brain (clogged, sluggish, running dry?) [870].

It's a sadomasochist's manifesto! Her self-sacrificing offer to sit at the bus stop whenever Grippes needed solitude was accompanied by her expressions of concern, each a poison dart aimed at his vulnerabilities in old age: the deterioration of his writing (as the critics had pointed out), his memory, his hearing, his brain. She had also offered to "sort his mail, tear up the rubbish, answer the telephone and the doorbell, and treat with sensitivity but firmness the floating shreds of his past" (870).

Grippes had taken "floating shreds" to mean his friend Mme. Obier and he had mounted a defense on her behalf. It was true that Mme. Obier, "convinced that any day was the ninth of September, 1980, and that Grippes was expecting her for tea, could make something of a nuisance of herself on the fourth-floor landing." But "think of the sixties," Grippes had pointed out, "when her flowing auburn hair and purple tights had drawn cheers in the Coupole" (870).

Now, the Coupole's renovated lighting, soft but revealing, "showed every crease and stain on the faces and clothes of the old crowd. Sociable elderly ladies, such as Mme. Obier, no longer roamed the aisles looking for someone to stand them a drink but were stopped at the entrance by a charming person holding a clipboard and wanting to know if they were expected" (871).

"A charming person with a clipboard" is a perfect symbol for the impersonal efficiency of the new era. With the passing of time, the legendary café and its former habitués, like Mme. Obier, have lost their identities. But if Mme. Obier was "a shred," Grippes had declared, she was "the fragment of a rich cultural past." And if she seemed old, it was only by comparison with Grippes, who not only looked younger than his age, but "from early youth … had always preferred the company of somewhat older women, immovably married to someone else…" (871).

The rest of his defense of Mme. Obier is less sympathetic. "Unfortunately, he had never foreseen the time when his friends, set loose because the husband had died or decamped … would start to scamper around Paris like demented ferrets. Having preceded Grippes in the field of life, they maintained an advance, beating him over the line to a final zone of"—and here he drops his sports metaphor and his mocking tone and gives a melancholy summation of the women's present state: "muddle, mistakes, and confused expectations" (871).

Grippes thinks now that perhaps he should have considered Mme. Parfaire's offer of "unpaid, unending, unflagging, serious-minded female service" (871). He had always eluded overtures to binding alliances, but the difference between Mme. Parfaire and other "applicants" was "in her confident grasp on time. She never mislaid a day or a minute." Grippes is beginning to experience the memory lapses of age, or as Gallant writes in a simple, moving sentence, "Grippes needs help with the past now" (872).

But, for the aging bachelor who has guarded his autonomy and whose cats (he has two at present) have provided companionship without infringing on his privacy, what is needed is "a competent assistant who can live in his head and sort out the archives. A resident inspiring goddess, a muse of a kind, created by Grippes, used to keep offhand order…" (871).

Gallant shows Grippes's aging, and his awareness of it, in understated, affecting ways. She notes that "no one dies in Grippes's novels; not any more" (872). She tells us that "he has left instructions that he is to be buried from the church of Notre Dame des Champs…. After all," Grippes had said, with a metaphoric shrug, "one has to be buried from somewhere" (872). And then there is his enigmatic dream or vision:

> Sometimes a long ribbon of sound unwinds in his sleep. He can see strangers, whole families, hurrying along an unknown street. Everything is gray-on-gray—pavement, windows, doorways, faces, clothes—under an opaque white sky. A child turns toward the camera—toward Grippes, the unmoving witness. Then, from a level still deeper than the source of the scene rises an assurance that lets him go on sleeping: None of this is real [874].

Is this a foreboding of death, followed by a temporary reprieve? The passage brings to mind the "freeze frame" that Gallant refers to in her description of her writing process: "the first flash of fiction [that] arrives without words," in which "the characters in the frame are not seen, but envisioned … and do not have to speak to be explained."[12] But, as it turns out, it was the wail of the air-raid siren with which this story began, and that Grippes, who was sleeping, had "wrapped up in a long dream" (874).

Later, at breakfast, he thinks of the war movies he saw in his youth and of his grandfather's farm, where his parents had sent him to live during the war. His recollection ends: "One afternoon Henri left the farm for good, dragging a suitcase with a broken lock, and got on a slow, dirty train to Paris" (874). The full import of this sentence is revealed nine pages later in Grippes's vivid recollection of the event that had precipitated his departure.

In the pocket of an old jacket Grippes has found a silver coffee spoon, a newspaper clipping, and an unopened letter addressed to him, with the words "Utopia Reconsidered" and a few scribbled sentences on the back of the envelope in his writing. Inside the envelope is the leaflet of a tenants' movement with a handwritten appeal to "Henri Grippes, whose published works and frequent letters to newspapers had always taken the side of the helpless" (876). These three items furnish Grippes (and Gallant) with enough material for five pages of associations, memories, and fantasies or, to draw on the music analogy again, inventive riffs.

Grippes sees that Mme. Parfaire's initials are engraved on the back of the silver coffee spoon. He has no idea how it got into his pocket and worries about his forgetfulness: "Only the other day, buying a newspaper, he had left it on the counter and started to walk off with another man's change. Apologizing, Grippes had said it was the first time he had ever done such an absentminded thing. Now he wondered if he ought to turn out the kitchen drawers and see how much in them really belonged to other people" (878). The spoon has other associations for Grippes too. It recalls the "abundant, well-cooked meals" in Mme. Parfaire's dining room upstairs, "a room that contained at all hours a rich and comforting smell of leek-and-potato soup" (878).

The scribbled sentences on the back of the tenants' envelope were the beginning of an overview of the early 1980s that Grippes had never finished. They bring back to him the "vision of Utopia" that "had occurred at eight in the evening on Sunday, the tenth of May, 1981, and had vanished ... at the same moment [when] a computerized portrait of François Mitterand, first Socialist president of the Fifth Republic, had unrolled on the television screen..." (877). Grippes had felt "stunned and deceived" even though "only a few hours before, he had cast his vote for precisely such an outcome." But he had voted "for a short list of principles, not their incarnation" (877). He had never expected his side to win.

"By temperament, by choice, ... by the cross-grained character of his profession he belonged in perpetual opposition. Now a devastating election result had made him a shareholder in power. No longer would he signify "minority rebellion" but "majority complacency," which might burden him with "majority responsibilities..." (877–8). "For the first time he had said to himself, 'I'm getting old for all this'" (879). Then, "reminded of the steadfast role of the writer in a restless universe," Grippes "had settled down to compose a position piece, keeping it as cloudy and imprecise as his native talent could make it" (880). In her description of Grippes's struggle to write, Gallant could have been describing the experience of all writers, especially aging ones, perhaps even the most fluent of them like herself: "Visions of perfection emerge and fade but the written word remains to trip the author who runs too fast for his time or lopes alongside at not quite the required pace" (880).

The next day Grippes had taken his article to "the most distinguished newspaper in France" who "had printed it, finally, not on page 1, with nationwide debate to follow, but on 2, the repository for unsolicited opinions too long-winded to pass as letters to the editor." A footnote had identified Grippes as "man of letters," which "confirmed his status and showed he was no amateur thinker" (880).

He rereads the article. "Now that the profit motive has been lopped from every branch of French cultural life," he had begun, but instead of continuing in that vein—perhaps with a vision of French cultural life liberated from the constraints of a market economy—Grippes had written what could have been the disgruntled letter of any old man (or old woman), complaining about the state of movie theaters, compared with "the old days" when "there was room for his legs" and when "he could place a folded jacket under the seat without having it stuck with gum."

"Now the capacious theater under Grippes's windows had been cut into eight small places, each the size of a cabin in a medium-haul jet....

Subtitles of foreign films dissolved in a white blur, while spoken dialogue could not be heard at all—at least not by Grippes." Then, as though suddenly remembering the occasion of his piece, Grippes had written in conclusion that "he knew that twenty-three years of right-wing government had produced a sullen and mumbling generation, but he felt sure that a drastic change, risen from the very depths of an ancient culture, would soon restore intelligible speech" (881).

"Last June, it rained every night" begins the next section of the story, with its abrupt change of time, place, and atmosphere. Gallant sets a cozy scene: it's three in the morning, Grippes is at his writing desk, the radio is playing soft jazz, a cat is sleeping under the desk lamp. Grippes gets up, pulls a book from the shelf and finds what he's looking for: a passage by "Jules Renard, dead for some eighty-odd years … quoted often by Grippes's father, dead now for more than forty." Grippes "had just written the last two sentences: same words, same order…. His inspiring goddess had found nothing better to dish up in the middle of the night than another man's journal, and even had the insolence to pass it off as original" (881–2).

His thoughts move from that sardonic reflection to a memory from his adolescence, which Gallant re-creates in a vivid flashback. It begins with the sound of a car: "The Renault, as it approached his grandfather's house, could be heard from a distance; it was a quiet afternoon, close to the end of things" (882). In Gallant's flashback, the quiet afternoon turns into a scene of violence and destruction when two plainclothes police get out of the car to search the house for contraband.

> [They] … turned up loose tiles and floorboards, slashed all the pillows and bolsters with a knife…. From the window of his wrecked bedroom … Henri watched the strangers digging aimlessly outside. They … threw the spades down and came back to the house. Their shoes left mud prints across the kitchen floor and up the scrubbed stairs [883].

The men, seen through Henri's eyes, are incompetent thugs whose contempt for the old people is made clear in two phrases of the last sentence: "mud prints" and "scrubbed stairs." Then they go into Henri's bedroom and one of them offers the boy an American cigarette. Grippes recalls the reaction of his younger self: "It was too precious to waste in smoke. He placed it carefully behind an ear and waited for the question. 'Where would you put a lot of contraband money, if you had any?' Henri answered, truthfully, 'In the dark and in plain sight'" (883).

His answer precipitates the climactic scene. Pushing Henri ahead of them, the men go down to the cellar, which is lined with shelves holding crocks of preserved fruit. They shine their flashlights on the shelves, where "in plain sight, every fourth crock was stuffed with gold coins and banknotes" (883). The men tell Henri to get a crate for the money, and he keeps count while they pack it up.

> [Henri] droned ... four, five, six ... while his grandmother wept.... Then he and his grandmother watched as the men handcuffed his grandfather and put him into the Renault. "Forgive me," said Henri. "I didn't know it was down there." "You had better be a long way from here before he gets back," his grandmother said [883].

This is the backstory that completes Grippes's memory of taking the train to Paris and leaving his grandparents' farm for good. Gallant, in using part of young Henri's answer to the plainclothes police about the location of the contraband—"In the dark and in plain sight"—for the title of this concluding story of the "Henri Grippes" sequence, seems to suggest that the encounter was a defining episode in Grippes's life.

It also suggests a serious defect in his character. We have seen that the adult Grippes is an opportunist and a schemer, and it's not difficult to imagine him guilty of a venial sin or two; but his unhesitating betrayal of his grandfather in exchange for a blackmarket American cigarette is a sin of a different order, and seems at odds with the flawed but engaging character that Gallant has created.

The morning after his recollections of the two policemen, Grippes is awakened by two policemen. Mme. Parfaire has reported intruders and they want to know if Grippes heard anything. Grippes thinks that the intruders are in her imagination. His view of her present state is a wickedly funny picture of Mme. Parfaire in old age:

> When she descends the curving staircase [she] clutches the banister, halts every few steps, wears a set expression. Strands of hair hang about her face.... She seems to be suffering from a wasting and undiagnosed fatigue of the nerves ... but it was clear to him that Mme. Parfaire was

doped to the eyes on tranquilizers, handed out in Paris like salted peanuts ... [884-5].

The final scene of the story is precipitated by the third object that Grippes found in the pocket of his old jacket: Mme. Parfaire's silver spoon. Grippes has thought of a plan to calm Mme. Parfaire's anxieties and to avail himself of her cooking. "Serving lunch would provide point and purpose to her day," he decides (886). He pictures "a plate of fresh mixed seafood with mayonnaise ... an omelette folded on a warmed plate, marinated herring and potato salad, a light ragout of lamb kidneys in wine" (886).

Then he pictures himself going into his study, where from the window he can see "the shadow of the Montparnasse tower.... Only yesterday, he started to tell himself—but no. A generation of Parisians had never known anything else" (886). This is the same tower that M. Wroblewski found so distressing and, like M. Wroblewski, Grippes is unsettled by all the changes in his Montparnasse neighborhood. But, unlike M. Wroblewski, Grippes is a pragmatist and quickly squelches any incipient stirrings of nostalgia for the past.

Now "an empty space ... occurred in his mind, somewhere between the sliding of the invitation—if one could call it that—under her door and the materialization of the omelette. The question was, How to fill the space?" It's the eternal question of the writer, and the irony is that Grippes wrestles with it while trying to compose a letter to Mme. Parfaire, for so long an object of his ridicule.

He tries, and rejects, various beginnings, then drifts into a briefly soothing, finally disillusioned fantasy:

> How good it would be to lie down on the kitchen floor and let his inspiring goddess kneel beside him, anxiously watching for the flutter of an eyelid, as he deftly lifts her wallet. But, like Grippes, ... his goddess is a victim of the times, hard up for currency and short of ideas [886-7].

In this, her last published story, Gallant wrote about the concerns of an aging writer: the failing memory, the drying up of ideas, the feeling of being out of step with the times. But her pace is so lively and her prose so witty and vigorous that, although the story is, de facto, an elegy, the tone is celebratory, not mournful.

8

Interview with Mavis Gallant

When Mavis Gallant agreed to my request to interview her in Paris on April 27, 2002, she wrote me that with any luck, the chestnut trees would begin to show their buds while I was there. But, thanks to global warming that had sent temperatures into the 70s and 80s, the chestnut trees and all the flowers and bushes were in full bloom when I arrived.

Gallant asked me to meet her at Le Dôme, a café in Montparnasse, her longtime neighborhood and the setting of many of her stories, including those discussed in this book. The oldest of the legendary gathering places for artists and writers who lived on the Left Bank, Le Dôme was now one of the best fish restaurants in Paris and Gallant treated me to Sunday lunch. We sat in the circular "Picasso booth," Gallant's usual spot, and I ate a simple, perfect meal that reminded me why the French are revered for their cooking.

Gallant, who would turn eighty-five in three months, seemed much younger, with her sharp mind, high, girlish voice, animated style of speaking, and frequent, rollicking laughter. She had brought the current issue of The New Yorker *to show me an article on old age by the doctor and writer, Atul Gawande, illustrated with a rather terrifying photograph by Richard Avedon of his father in extreme old age. I asked Gallant what she thought was the purpose of the photograph. "To scare us all," she replied instantly, "That is its purpose!" and burst into one of her rollicking laughs.*

Esther Harriott: When you left your job as a journalist at the Montreal Standard **and moved to Europe to write fiction full-time, did you know that your great subject would be the effects of the Second World War on the lives of Europeans?**

Mavis Gallant: No, I had no idea. I just wanted to know what had happened. I wanted the truth about Spain because it was my first political experience. I still remember when the Civil War was declared. I was in Canada, just going to be fourteen, and I remember the faces of the grownups. Very grave. And all the people I ever met or knew in my adolescence were anti-Franco.

Harriott: You became politically aware at a very young age. That was unusual, wasn't it, especially for a girl?

Gallant: Especially for a girl. I know that now. And later in my adolescence, when I lived in New York, I would go by myself to a couple of bookstores. I never belonged to a group and I had no mentor, so I was working all this out alone in my mind. There was a bookstore called the Little Lenin Library and I bought books with my pocket money. And when I came to Europe—don't forget I was a journalist—I wanted to find out certain things that I hadn't been able to find out in my interviews with refugees in Canada. People who have been victims can't tell you about the people who victimized them. They can only say "It was a brute."

Harriott: They don't analyze.

Gallant: No. They don't want to. What happened was the greatest tragedy of the century. There was nothing to compare. The Soviet Union went into Auschwitz and filmed what they saw and took the films back to Moscow. After the war they released pictures, not of the prisoners but of heaps of human hands and suitcases, things like that. Nobody had ever seen such things before. Now they've been so clichéd that it makes you want to cry. I did mention that in the story about the actor.

Harriott: Gabriel Baum?

Gallant: "Baum, Gabriel," yes, about how after the war they made this stuff into viewing for television. And Gabriel's friend says that there'll be a call for this sort of thing until about 1982, so they should take advantage of it while they can. And finally Gabriel is told that he's too old to play a Jew.

Harriott: And he is a Jew. That irony does what it's supposed to do. No matter how ironic your stories are, they're compassionate too.

Gallant: Do you think so? They're often accused of just the opposite.

Maybe because of their ironic tone. And you can be devastating in your portrayal of stupid behavior. But you were the first writer who wrote about the suffering of Germans during and after the war. German writers didn't write about it because they felt they didn't have the right to.

I wasn't looking to be compassionate. I was looking for answers. I had a high regard for German culture—the music, the poetry—and I wanted to find out why this had not stood up to the extreme philistine content of the Nazi rule. The only way I could do it was if I worked like a reporter. I took notes.

You gave up journalism for fiction, but in your fiction you show a reporter's eye for detail.

Yes, somebody told me that, an American poet. She had me meet her young daughter and while we were having lunch, I asked her daughter a lot of questions. Her mother was amused and afterwards she said, "You're *still* a reporter."

I keep coming across stories of yours that weren't in the Collected Stories. *There are three of them in your collection* Varieties of Exile, *including one that was never published before, anywhere.*

The *Collected Stories?* It's only half. It shouldn't be called "Collected." Luckily for me, in England and in Canada the editors agreed that it should be the "Selected." But in America, the tradition is to use "Collected." The editor explained this attitude to me. He said that if you call it "Selected Stories," people wouldn't be interested. They'd think, "Well, what about the other ones?"

What about *the other ones, by the way? Is it possible that New York Review Books might publish them?*

They've already done two books, *Paris Stories* and *Varieties of Exile*.

How did that come about?

I've no idea.

I wondered if the first one was Michael Ondaatje's endeavor.

I think they asked Michael if he would do a preface, which he did, beautifully.

And Russell Banks did the second volume.

Yes. I was very moved that they would take time off from their own work, because their work is important. And they had to read a great deal. They weren't just presented with the stories and told to write an introduction. They chose them.

So it was Russell Banks who chose to make a collection of Canadian stories. I thought it was interesting that the book was called Varieties of Exile *and all the stories in it were set in Canada.*

It was to be—and I wanted it to be—called *Montreal Stories*. That is what it's called in Canada. "Varieties of Exile" is the title of one of the stories, but I didn't want it as the title of the book. I get sick of reading that I write only about exiles. Show me where I've written about exiles in it. If you move from British Columbia to Nova Scotia, are you an exile? No, you're in your own country. It's not exile; it's a choice.

The stories in the Collected *were written from the 1950s through the 1990s and, unless I look up when each story was published, I can't guess the decade in which it was written.*

Are you talking about the way they are grouped in decades? That was *my* idea. I didn't want them in chronological order according to when I wrote them, which is of no interest to anyone as far as I could see. They were grouped according to the decade in which they were set. Not everyone understood this. There were actually people who thought that I was writing the stories in "The Thirties" in the thirties. I was born in the twenties. I was precocious, but not that precocious!

What I meant is that, unless I look up the date that a story was first published, I can't tell whether you wrote it in the fifties or the nineties. Your writing has been at the same level throughout your career. There hasn't been a falling off in the later work, or early work that wasn't very good. No one would say, "Oh, that's obviously her early work." You seemed to begin as a fully formed writer. That voice was there from the start, from your very first story.

"Madeleine's Birthday."

"Madeleine's Birthday?" I don't remember a story with that title. Oh, but it's not in the Collected.

It's not in any of the collections. But I have a special feeling for that story.

I'd love to read it. I'm hungry for more of your stories and I'm sure there are a lot of other readers who feel the same way.

There wouldn't be a lot. Be careful. There wouldn't be a lot. There'd be some.

You probably didn't imagine such an enthusiastic reception for the stories that were published in the Collected, *did you?*

No, and it was very reassuring to me to see the reviews, because they were reviewing a whole lifetime of work. Nobody said, "She has wasted our time and wasted her own." [*Laughs*] But they were very touching.

I haven't seen a bad review of your work.

I haven't either, but maybe there were.

You don't get bad reviews, just admiring ones. But the thing that I find so difficult to understand is why you aren't better known generally.

I think if you write short stories you're not as well known as if you write novels. People don't like reading a volume of short stories or they try to read them like chapters of a novel, and you can't. I have read Chekhov's stories many, many times—there is always a volume hanging around—and after I read one, I put the book away.

Is it true in France, too, that people don't read short stories as much as they read novels?

It's true the whole world over. But people go on writing them. [*Laughs*] I remember being interviewed once in Rome—it was a very young interviewer—and he said that every journalist in Italy has a short story in his drawer.

Well, be that as it may, I think it's especially egregious that your work wasn't published in Canada until 1981, the same year that they gave you the Governor General's award, your first Canadian award. Do you think there was resentment that you didn't come back to Canada?

Do you mean come back to live? I never intended to.

I know that it wasn't unusual for Canadian writers to leave Canada for England or the United States or France—they had to leave in order to get published and become recognized. Morley Callaghan left, Morde-

cai Richler left, Margaret Atwood left. But then they came back. You didn't.

Well, Mordecai is the only one I can speak for because he's the only one I know and we did talk about it. He loved England, you know, he loved living there. But you should be able to describe the people among whom you live and he told me that he reached a point where he could not bring to life British characters. He said to me, "If a Canadian crosses the room to get a cigarette, I know what he's doing and I know why he's doing it. But if a Brit walks across the room, I don't know what he's doing."

That's certainly a great gift of yours—bringing to life characters of many different nationalities. In "The Pegnitz Junction" Christine listens to the memories of the German woman on the train about the years that she and her family had lived in Elmhurst, Queens, of all places. How were you able to write, and in such intimate detail, about their habits and attitudes? You seemed to have an astonishing amount of information about her day-to-day life. And you never lived there, did you?

I did live in New York for a time, you know, as an adolescent. I didn't live in Queens. There was a time when it was a German center. Ethnic Germans lived there. It isn't now, it wasn't when I wrote it either. But I could imagine them, having been to Germany a lot. And I had heard about people like these two couples who come from Germany and they see only each other all the time they're there. Their children go out and make friends, but they never see anybody except these people from their hometown in Germany.

When I read "The Pegnitz Junction," I thought to myself that Christine, the narrator, is like you. She has special antennae that can tune into the voices of all kinds of people.

I think it's the best thing I ever did. I couldn't go on along that line because you can't keep repeating. It would become very boring. You can do that once—satirizing the history, the culture, the literature. Obviously that family going to visit the castle on top of a hill is from Kafka's novel *The Castle*. But in "The Pegnitz Junction" when they get up there, all they want is to go to the bathroom.

"The Pegnitz Junction" wasn't published in* The New Yorker, *was it?

No. William Maxwell [Gallant's first and longtime editor at *The New Yorker*] said it was too long. But when he was in his nineties and rereading the work of various writers he had published, he read "The Pegnitz Junction" in the published book. And this time he wrote me a letter that I don't think any editor has ever written a writer because, you know, no editor is going to say, "I made a mistake." But he did. He said, "My critical faculties must have been out to lunch." He also said, "I didn't realize how much was meant to be funny."

Your stories* are *funny. I'm surprised that he didn't get that.

Another thing was that he wasn't crazy about Germany. He'd had two world wars and the horror of the revelations after the second one. Also, he was very caught up at that time with the notion of *The New Yorker* short story, which was linear. One thing he had said to me was that my stories went round and round.

Your stories aren't nonlinear in the postmodern sense. Time shifts from present to past the way it would in a novel. Reading your long stories and your linked stories is like reading a novel.

They're squashed novels. [*Laughs*]

And now you're working on your journals for publication?

It's a huge job and I don't know if I'm good for a dime, but I want to be the one to do it.

Are these the journals where you kept the notes that you later turned into stories?

I never actually went back and looked things up. I may have gone back and looked to make sure I had the sequence right, because one thing you don't remember, I've discovered, is exactly what sequence of time things happened in. You think that you talked to so-and-so and it was a very important conversation about a certain event, and then you go back and find, no, it wasn't important at all, and it took place months before the event. The publisher is Canadian and I think they could only be published in Canada because in America they would want one book. I would be expected to troll through fifty years and give them nuggets.

8—Interview with Mavis Gallant

Do they also contain your memoirs?

No, it's what you write at the end of the day. Diaries. Journals. You write, "The greatest cellist in the world died today." *[Gallant was referring to the cellist Mstislav Rostropovich, who died April 27, 2007, the day of the interview.]* But I don't keep them as carefully now. As you grow older, I think you write more in your letters to people.

Has anybody suggested a "Collected Letters?"

Not by me, I can tell you. After I die they can do as they like with my letters.

I was thinking of the published correspondence between William Maxwell and Sylvia Townsend Warner.

They each kept each other's letters. Tons and tons of letters. I sent him some letters that she had written me—I had never met her—so he could choose. Only one was worth publishing and that is in the introduction. But he didn't send them all back and I didn't want to trouble him. I only have about one now that he sent back.

Was that just negligence or carelessness?

Yes, carelessness. His desk at home was just heaped. Mine is a mess, but nothing compared to his.

You told me that the main difference that you find in writing now is that it's slower.

Physically. It's not mental. Don't forget, I'm going to be eighty-five this summer. It's a great age.

I know that you are "pestered by osteoporosis," as you once wrote me, but you seem to have a tremendous amount of energy. And you're extremely sharp.

I'll tell you what the differences are in writing now. They're physical. I have trouble with my hands. I'm going to pick this up [*picks up a swizzle stick as if it were a pen*] and put it there [*she curves the thumb and index finger on her right hand so that it forms an "o"*] and if I'm going to write, I put the pen through here and then write like this.

No wonder your writing is slower. Your fingers are put into such an awkward position.

I've just had the proofs from an Italian collection that's coming out in June and I had to write the preface. And the translator—a very good translator, a very sharp young woman—said that my J's looked like L's to her. I was writing about a character in a story by Anatole France whose name was "Jeanne," and she had put "Leanne" all the way through. I could just imagine the indignation of one of Anatole France's devoted readers. [*Gallant acts out, in voluble French, the reader's indignation.*]

[Laughing] By the way, your story "The Concert Party" made me laugh out loud. Will that be in the Italian book?

There are three linked stories—"Let It Pass," "In the War," and "The Concert Party." "The Concert Party" is far and away the best. I don't argue with editors because I don't sell books. I'm not in that business. But if I had been choosing out of the three, I would have taken "The Concert Party."

Which did they choose?

They chose the first one, "Let It Pass," which is from a quotation from Scott Fitzgerald. "Let it pass, he thought. April is over, April is over. There are all kinds of love in the world but never the same love twice." [*Laughs*] It's from a story called "All the Sad Young Men" and I used it as an epigraph. The Italian editor liked that one better than "The Concert Party." I didn't insist. I insisted on the title when *The Pegnitz Junction* was first published as a book with the German stories. It was Random House in New York and I insisted on having that as the title. That's why I don't insist on anything now. The sales department or whatever they call it objected. They said it was an absolutely lousy title for an American book. "No, no, no!" I said. They gave in to me, and people couldn't pronounce "Pegnitz," they couldn't remember it, "Pegnitz Junction" was hard to say, they didn't know what it was about. And it barely sold. After that, I thought, I'm out of this. One reason I insisted was that I hadn't insisted on changing the title "My Heart Is Broken." I hated that for a book. It's the title of a story, but that's different. It's about a girl who's been raped in the north woods of Quebec and she's talking about it to the wife of another engineer at this logging camp. She says, "He didn't even *like* me." And then she says, "My heart is broken, you know. My heart is *just* broken."

8—Interview with Mavis Gallant

A lot of your stories have dramatic scenes in them. I'm thinking of, for example, "Four Seasons," when the two English maiden ladies come to visit and the clergyman drops in. The story is sad, but this one scene is like a drawing room comedy by Oscar Wilde. I loved the way you satirized the two Englishwomen.

I lived down there, on the Riviera, and got to know why [*laughing*] India rebelled.

You are always sympathetic, even tender, to children and to the young servants of the English expatriates on the Riviera, like Angelo, in "An Unmarried Man's Summer."

The boy, Angelo—I saw that! About every second Englishman is gay, as you know.

No, I didn't know. They certainly sound it in your stories. I thought that Englishmen being gay was a French prejudice.

Oh, no. They lived in the South of France, where they were free. In England, as in Canada, it was a criminal offense. They could go to the penitentiary. But they got down there and had a field day with Italian boys from poor families, whose lives were then perverted forever. In that case you can say "perverted" because it was forced on them. When Walter's sister tells him that Angelo eyes the girls on the beach, he says, "Well, I'm not stopping him." But he *was*.

Does it get harder to write fiction—to make up stories—as you get older?

What I find is that if I don't write down *at once* what occurs to me in the way of fiction, it is gone. I used to be able to keep it in mind, as if I had a filing cabinet in my brain, and I don't any more. There's no point in trying to do it two days later. I would not now attempt in fiction things that I hadn't seen in years. When I wrote *Green Water, Green Sky*, which was a novel that I wrote in the fifties, I was very close to the way Americans lived. I could, with great confidence, get into an American family, an American mother and daughter, and so forth. I couldn't do that now. If there was going to be a mother-and-daughter squabble, they would have to be French or Canadian, even British. I haven't lost track of my American friends, but I *have* lost track of the way they live. I don't know what they have in their kitchens any more. Everything seems to be extraordinarily modern and beyond me. [*Laughs*]

In the eighties I spent a year in Toronto as writer-in-residence at the U of T [University of Toronto] and I accepted it only because it would give me some experience of daily life in English Canada, which I'd lost track of. When you see your friends you don't say, "How do you make your toast in the morning? Is it still the way it used to be?" I still feel confident about French Canada, but not as much as before the revolutions in the sixties and seventies. So I would stay away from something unless I was absolutely sure that I wasn't going to fall flat on my face, whereas before I didn't have that worry. I'd have it all filed away.

So memory plays a role that way, but you don't have difficulty with words? They don't disappear?

Oh, yes, but not constantly. It happens and then you just sit there until you get the circuit tied up again. I think of it as a thread that's broken somewhere, and I will just sit there stubbornly until I get it back, going over the alphabet—a, b, c, d—so that the word will jump out at some point. It's usually a name more than a word.

How do you choose the names of your characters? They seem particularly well-suited to them.

They appear with their own names. This happened with *Green Water, Green Sky*. The one who was eventually called Florence I had named Caroline. Well, I had just that year been godmother to a little girl. They named her Caroline and I thought, "She's going to grow up and read this and think it's about her." But I had to write the novel with it. If I changed names, I lost the whole thing. And when it was all done and all ready to be set up in proof, then I went over it with a pencil and wherever it said "Caroline" I crossed it out and put in "Florence." But I couldn't have written her as "Florence." She'd have been someone else. It's hard to explain. People recognize themselves even if they're not in it. My ex-husband used to recognize himself in everyone, even the women. [*Laughs*]

[Laughs] He must have been rather self-centered.

There was a story called "Autumn Day" that takes place in Austria during the occupation after the war. And *there* I was sure of my ground because I lived for some months on a farm outside Salzburg where they rented rooms, and I could still confidently do Americans in the fifties. And in "Autumn Day," a very young American woman, an army wife, is stuck in this same place. She tells the story and she says, "I was eighteen when I married Walt and I was twenty when we went to occupied Austria with the army." My ex-husband read the first line and he told me that I wasn't eighteen when we married, I was nineteen when we met and I was twenty when we married. He said, "I put it down and swallowed a big glass of cold water, and then I read the rest of it, and then I decided it wasn't us." And, much to his disappointment, I said, "I have never written about you, even remotely." He seemed a bit miffed.

You wrote in your Linnet Muir stories that your father, who died at thirty-one, had always thought of himself as a painter and that it may have been just as well that he didn't go on to discover that he could never have been more than a dedicated amateur. And that left you with the fear that you may have inherited his legacy of a sense of vocation without the ability to sustain it.

Yes, I thought perhaps I didn't have the talent for it.

You alluded to that fear when you read in New York last fall, and you said you were seventy-six before you felt you had succeeded. The friend sitting beside me, who has read all of your work, whispered to me in disbelief, "How is that possible? How could she think that?" So: how is that possible?

I don't know. I thought that perhaps I didn't have the talent for what I wanted to do. But I think that anyone who is overly sure probably isn't very good. On the other hand, you have to have a belief in yourself or you wouldn't throw up a job and go live in Europe.

I was going to say that you certainly demonstrated a fierce belief in yourself.

Yes, on the upper surface of things. I'd think, "This is all right this week, but what about next week? Maybe I won't be able to write another word." I felt this with the preface I just finished writing for the Italian book. What if my mind has got sclerosis, you know, because I haven't written anything like this for a while—an introduction to my own work.

You wrote the afterword to* Paris Stories *in 2002 and it was beautiful.
That was my introduction to the *Collected Stories* and they just took it and used it as the afterword. And that was a few years ago. But I read the introduction to the Italian stories and it seemed to work. It's called "Memory and Imagination."

You've said that when you reread some of your earlier work now, you can see which writers were influencing you at the time. Who were they? Was Chekhov one of them?
Oh, strongly. Elizabeth Bowen was one. And E. M. Forster.

No Americans? I think I read that you like Eudora Welty.
Oh, I *love* Eudora Welty. I began reading her in my early twenties. I think I read everything she ever wrote. But I don't think she influenced my writing.

You mentioned your novel* Green Water, Green Sky. *Reading it as a novel and then reading the chapter from it that became the short story "August" is a completely different, and I think more powerful, experience. Flor's breakdown on the sidewalk is almost visceral.
I had a Spanish friend, who was a difficult friend to have because she talked only about herself and her mental states. She told me the thing about the sidewalk breakdown. I told her I was going to use it in the story and she said, "I'd better look at it," and then she said, "That's right."

The characters in that story are all very real.
Well, I was closer to Americans then. I knew people like that.

And their remarks about Flor's Jewish husband that aren't* quite *anti-Semitic are exactly right.
Listen, I'll tell you. This was going to be translated into French, which it was, and life had changed. There was anti-Semitism in France. This was after Auschwitz. People weren't as conscious of things they were saying that could be offensive. I gave the proofs in French to a friend and I said to her, "You were in Auschwitz, your husband died in the camp near Vienna. Is there anything in it that makes you withdraw?" And she called me after she'd read it and said no, "*Il n'y a rien.*" I looked a lot for survivors when I was trying to find out what happened. She was

the only one who had a sort of black humor about her life and about Germans. She had her tattoo on her arm and in summer she wore short sleeves and this thing blazoned in peacock blue on her arm and she'd be absolutely unselfconscious about it. We'd be in restaurants and people would look at her and there was a kind of hostility sometimes.

At her for displaying it?
Yes.

As though it was in bad taste.
Once we were in Coupole having a meal and there were two German couples sitting near us. And she said to me, in French, without lowering her voice at all, "The men are going to order two desserts, but the women will only order one because they don't want to get fat." And they did. I said, "How did you know?" and she said. "How do *I* know about the Germans?"

She used irony to save her feelings.
Oh, she was constantly ironic. Sometimes she had to be warned. She was an artist and she had taught in a German *gymnasium* before the war. I asked her if she had taught art and she said, "No, no, I taught the language and…" and then she paused and said dramatically *[Gallant also pauses and says dramatically]* "The Civilization."

You wrote a lot of stories about the Germans and Poles who emigrated to France after the war.
Yes, because I knew them. I went into all these people who were here post-war. Nobody wrote about them. The Polish were a vivid émigré group and gave me a false idea of Poland. There was no anti–Semitism, no anti-anything. They were writers, they were painters, and they saw each other all the time. They went to each other's exhibitions and readings. But I'm seeing what's going on in Poland now. It's serious, terrible. They're right back in the 1930s. But if you knew only the intellectuals, it was an ideal society.

Like the Polish writers in "Forain." The main character, Tremski, is a Jew, but he and the other Polish émigré writers are devoted to each other.
But then there's the young woman at the end who comes out of Poland later and becomes the publisher's assistant, Forain's assistant,

and she doesn't speak the same language as the Poles who came earlier. I thought that would be interesting, but people didn't get it. The one who loved those Polish stories is a Canadian writer, Janice Kulyk Keefer. She's half–Polish and half–Ukrainian, and she read the two Polish stories I had put in *The New Yorker*. She loved that story and the story about the Polish man whose wife has Alzheimer's. He's in Paris and he's corresponding with someone who's in Poland.

"A State of Affairs."

Yes. I ran into her at one of those things where you all run into each other, and she said, "You got it right."

That's exactly it. You get it right!

Afterword

A few months after interviewing Gallant, I came across her review of Secrets of the Flesh, *a biography of Colette, that had appeared in* The New York Times *on October 17, 1999. I was struck, and moved, by its two last sentences:* "[Colette] had written steadily from her early twenties until her mid-seventies, when she had to stop. Her hand was frozen in a permanent writer's cramp and could no longer hold a pen." *Eight years after Gallant wrote those sentences, they had become an accurate description of her own hand, frozen into the permanent "O" that she had demonstrated in Le Dôme. In Gallant's case, the frozen hand was caused by the osteoporosis that had also bent her back in two, that was making it increasingly difficult for her to walk, and that she never complained about or allowed to interfere with her high spirits.*

9

Russell Baker

On December 25, 1998, *The New York Times* published the last "Observer," the column by Russell Baker that had appeared in the *Times* (and its syndicated papers) since July 16, 1962. The understated, almost offhand tone with which Baker began his valedictory column made the announcement of his departure even more poignant for the millions of people (myself among them) for whom the "Observer" had become indispensable reading.

"Since it is Christmas, a day on which nobody reads a newspaper anyway," he wrote, "and since this is the last of the columns titled 'Observer' which have been appearing in the Times since 1962, I shall take the otherwise inexcusable liberty of talking about me and newspapers. I love them."[1] Then, with an economy perfected over almost four decades of writing a 700-word column twice a week (three times a week until the Sunday "Observer" ended in 1988), Baker wrote a farewell letter to newspapers that was also a brief, funny, and affecting memoir of his long association with them.

The association began in his childhood, when "Uncle Allen regularly brought home Hearst's New York Journal-American," with its comics, cartoons, and "tales of rich playboys, murderous playgirls, and their love nests." The tales fascinated the boy, even if he didn't know (and he didn't ask) what "love nests" were. On Sundays, Uncle Allen brought *The New York Times*, which the future writer for that newspaper evaluated as "a dismal mass of gray paper ... which was of absolutely no interest to me."

But at his friend Harry's, he discovered the New York tabloids, which had "lots of great pictures, Dick Tracy, and stories about condemned killers being executed, with emphasis on what they had eaten for their last meal, before walking—the last mile!"

Later, when he "inevitably ... was admitted to practice the trade,"

Baker marveled at the places newspapers could take him—to "suburbs on sunny Saturday afternoons to witness the mortal results of family quarrels in households that kept pistols" and to "hospital emergency rooms to listen to people die and to ogle nurses."

Later still, they took him to more exotic destinations—like the Elysée Palace, where he "gazed on the grandeur that was Charles de Gaulle speaking as from Olympus," and Iran, where he rode in a press bus "over several miles of Oriental carpets with which the Shah had ordered the street covered between airport and town to honor the visiting President Eisenhower."

The last paragraph of the column was as succinct as the first. "I could go on and on, and probably will somewhere sometime," Baker wrote, "but the time for this enterprise is over. Thanks for listening for the past three million words."

"Listening" was the perfect word. The "Observer" always seemed to speak directly to the reader, either in Baker's voice, which was genial and ironic, or in the voice of one of his invented personae, who "talked" the column under Baker's unobtrusive direction. And the three million words cohered into an astute eyewitness report of American society during the last half of the twentieth century.

In Baker's view, it was a period of breakdown that began in the 1960s and worsened in each succeeding decade, and it could be observed in every area of American life, from the despoliation of the landscape to the depredations of the language; the collapse of education aimed at civilizing people and the arrival of television and the end of conversation; the increasing importance of money and the decreasing concern for the poor and the powerless. Baker's genius was to write about this breakdown in a consistently entertaining way. Like one of his literary ancestors, Mark Twain, he was a sophisticated satirist with broad popular appeal, but unlike Twain, Baker did not become embittered in his later years. Even when his satire was scathing, he got away with it because of the charm and playfulness of his writing style.

Baker's theme—an examination of the society he lived in—was serious, but his approach was humorous. He didn't scold; he spoofed. And his mastery of the fictional devices of storytelling, dialogue, and portraiture made the "Observer" fun to read and its hints of anger to go unnoticed. It was only when I read the published collections of the columns as a body of work that I became aware of the melancholy strain underneath their funny surfaces.

There was one subject that Baker never satirized: his roots in Morristown, Virginia, where he was born in 1925. He was only five years old when his father died and Baker and his mother moved to Baltimore to live with his mother's relatives. But the tiny rural community where he spent his earliest years surrounded by members of his father's extended family remained in Baker's memory and imagination as a permanent image of home.

In a column called "A Summer Beyond Wish," he wrote about a summer day in this village of "seven houses of varying lack of distinction," where he "enjoyed innocence and never knew boredom, although nothing of consequence happened there."[2] Writing in lyrical, unsentimental prose, Baker makes you feel the day's rhythms and the reassurance of its unvarying patterns, from the "early-morning hubbub of women," cleaning and polishing kerosene lamps, to the hot mid-afternoon, "when the women would draw the blinds [and] spread blankets on the floor for coolness and nap," to sunset, when people sat on their porches and "as dusk deepened, the lightning bugs came out to be caught and bottled" (a small boy's view of the purpose of lightning bugs).

One night, when the children were allowed to stay outside after dark, they saw a shooting star and "someone said, 'Make a wish.'" Baker recalls his response: "I did not know what that meant. I did not know anything to wish for." Those two short sentences that end the piece convey the child's view and the man's memory of the perfection of those days, that life. And, like his satirical sketches of American society, Baker's evocations of his Edenic childhood were laments for a vanished America that was better than the America he lived in now.

On Growing Old

Baker turned sixty-five in 1990, so that the beginning of the last decade of the "Observer" corresponded with the (official) beginning of Baker's old age. It was also the decade in which the oldest baby boomers, the huge generation born between 1946 and 1964, reached fifty and, as an observer of American society, Baker wrote more about their aging than his own. The boomers had created their own culture, one that glorified youth ("Don't trust anyone over thirty" was their famous mantra), and Baker was certain that they would also try to create their own culture of age, one that would reject the definitions and attitudes of earlier generations.

His columns about the aging boomers, like his other columns in the 1990s, were as fresh and funny as ever, but they revealed more of the anger that lies behind satire and showed Baker's disgust with the excesses of "The Decadent Decade" (the title of his column about the new class of the super-duper-rich, as distinguished from the merely superrich). There were occasional outbursts of moral indignation, as in his otherwise funny "Saps of Today and Yesterday," in which Baker wrote, "Today's boomers now confront a world of their own making which cannot much comfort their spirits. What do they see? A society ruled by greed and moral license. A nation whose governing political theory is devil-take-the-hindmost."[3]

Then, as though to apologize for losing his temper, he immediately offered a self-deprecatory explanation: "All the above, I hasten to say, is the kind of highly doubtful speculation we fall into when generalizing about decades, generational antipathies and the flow of history. I hope no one will swallow it whole."

"No Place for Crybabies"

Baker wrote about his own aging in "No Place for Crybabies," but he addressed the column to the baby-boomer generation, which was "looking down the gun barrel of fifty and worried about what to expect. At its request," he explained, "I have gone ahead to scout the territory."[4] What followed was a tongue-in-cheek report of his reactions as he revisited each of his birthdays, from the fiftieth to the seventy-third (his own age at the time).

Baker's report from his fiftieth birthday is jubilant: "You wake feeling wonderful. This is because you are still alive. Not only still alive, you also feel exactly the way you felt yesterday. What joy! Now that you've crossed the great divide, you could very well live forever!" But by the time (eleven reports later) that Baker has reached his sixty-first birthday, he is feeling the first signs of anxiety about his cognitive powers, an anxiety to which he responds with comic bravado: "The old drain—brain, that is—has it ever been sharper, more alert, quicker to grasp Frankenstein's theory of relativity or coin a side-splitting catechism—solecism?—prism?—fanaticism?—Manicheanism?—what's the word I'm looking for?" The monosyllabic report from his sixty-second birthday—"Witticism"—brings to a close his long search for the vanished word that is so familiar after a certain age.

The sequence continues as Baker greets each successive birthday and its accompanying new signs of age with good-humored self-mockery, but his tone changes on his seventy-second birthday with its irrefutable confirmation of the old age of a parent: "What's this! The children's hair gray? It makes you feel old for the first time." The seventy-third offers its ironic consolation: "How wonderful being old enough to see your teen-age grandchildren abuse your children the way your children used to abuse you." This concluded Baker's report for the time being. "More after I scout further ahead," he promises the boomers.

"Fooling with Faces"

"No Place for Crybabies" was Baker fooling around. "Fooling with Faces" was Baker fooling around with serious intent. He begins with a droll account, much of it at his own expense, of a recent bookselling tour, which included his appearances on TV. When he arrived at the television station, he tells us, a young woman "commanded, 'Take him to makeup'" in a manner that "made it clear she wanted nothing to do with me, or my book, until I had been taken to makeup."[5]

Another young woman took him to makeup, where a third woman seated him, studied his face, "sighed the sigh of a woman who has to put up with a lot, and started burying my face under powders and creams." Realizing what she was up to, Baker asked, "Why are you robbing my face of all its character?" He was hoping that his question might stop her before she took his face back to age twenty-two. "I have been twenty-two and have no wish to revisit the territory," he tells us, "especially when I am expected to go on television, boast about the excellence of my book, and urge millions to read it." At twenty-two he lacked the "unlimited supplies of gall" that such an act requires.

He adds that his face has become far more interesting since then, and supports his claim by quoting critical opinion: "'Haggard' and 'ravaged,' some critics have called it. 'Like well-aged leather,' said another." Baker assures us that this is not a boast. "The country has millions of faces that are just as interesting.... Not many of them, however, are twenty-two years old." And yet, as he continued making his bookselling rounds of television studios, he was "constantly taken to makeup, where cosmeticians toiled to make me a new face that was as young and uninteresting as the cosmetic art can create."

Baker lists the various reasons that have been given for television's insistence on young faces: "American youth fantasies, popular fear of aging, television's preference for the unreal, sponsors' financial need to pander to audiences," and adds that most of these reasons "originated in a time when the big baby-boomer population was youthful and television giddy with eagerness to exploit our darling young." He notes that "over the next ten years the boomers will be coming to grips with the reality of aging," whose physical signs he describes, with a pointed lack of word-mincing, as "the thickened waist, blurring vision, loosening teeth, surly innards—all those challenges of real life that television still tries to make them look upon with dread and contempt."

The irony—and Baker's serious point—is that "the boomers have been moving on toward wrinkles and stiff joints, while the networks continue sending everybody to makeup for the face of youth."

"Don't Believe It, Kids"

To his target of television's false images of age, Baker added his long-time target of politically correct speech, now directed at the aging baby boomers. "We will soon be inundated with nonsense about how wonderful it is to be old," he writes. "The baby-boom generation, now becoming long in the tooth, thick in the middle and sparse on the scalp will demand it. And who has ever been foolish enough to deny this vast army of demanders anything it calls for?

"Now that it is becoming an army of old crocks, everyone will be forbidden to say 'old crocks.' Saying 'old crocks' will be politically incorrect and punishable by social exile," and, with a retroactive dig at the boomers, adds, "just as these new arrivals in the land of Old Crockdom once exiled their elders for being 'over 30.' The word 'dotage' will also be stricken from the language when discussing people who have trouble remembering other people's names."[6]

Baker recalls that "the last attempt to gussy up the language about old age produced the embarrassingly insincere 'senior citizen' ... cooked up during the 1950s ... by advertising men...." (That attempt, "embarrassingly insincere" as it was, was successful: more than a half-century after the invention of the phrase, its abbreviated form, "seniors," is commonly—even officially—used when referring to the old.)

He alerts the boomers to a recent example of gussied-up language: the slogan of an advertising campaign on television "declaring that this is 'a great time to be silver.'" The silver in this slogan is not clearly defined, he says, but he assumes that it means gray hair. The product being advertised is a vitamin pill, which "obviously works wonders," because even though the actors "having a great time being silver ... still look young enough to run the Boston marathon ... they are actually, like Dorian Gray, far into the Social Security years."

As one who "still thinks of baby boomers as kids," Baker continues, "I don't want them marching into the new century under the delusion that old age is wonderful. It's not half as bad as it's cracked up to be, but wonderful it is not." To find out the truth about old age, he advises the boomers to "check the network news shows right away before advertisers revise everything to prove that senility is glorious." Because the news is "watched exclusively by graybeards nowadays," Baker explains, their commercials are "aimed at selling real-life old crocks the stuff that helps them make it through the day."

"And what are they offered?" Just as he deliberately used the unlovely phrases "old crocks" and "graybeards" for their contrast with the seductively worded lies of politically correct speech, Baker now makes a list of medications for some of the more repulsive ailments of old age: "Nostrums for relieving diarrhea, constipation, insomnia and disorders of the gastrointestinal tract. Adhesives for keeping dentures in place. Diapers for coping with incontinence."

Reminding the boomers that every stage of life has its drawbacks, he reviews the earlier ones, emphasizing their worst aspects. "Childhood ... is a prison existence"; "adolescence is pure horror: pimples, sexual panic, fear of unpopularity...." Then "twenty years of keeping up with the Joneses, impressing the boss, being untrusted by the kids because you're over thirty..." and on to "midlife with its famous crisis, despair, disappointment, suspicion that life has been wasted."

In conspicuously non–PC phrases, Baker points out some of the overlooked advantages of old age: "One of the many rewards for making it to the top of Mount Dotage is the fresh angle of vision that comes from standing up there on the top.... The land of Old Crockdom has surprising compensations, one of which is the right to say that being in your dotage excuses you from the obligation to remember who Brad Pitt is, or to care." Old age liberates us from having to keep up with the latest new movie star (or latest new anything) in order to appear with-it, i.e., young.

It liberates us from much more than that. "Crockhood means no longer having to do most of the things you never really wanted to do when you still thought that doing them could make each stage of life wonderful at last," Baker writes. But the last half of that sentence adds a note of ambiguity: is he referring to age's clear-eyed view or to its disillusionment?

Hunting That Fountain

The fountain is, of course, the fountain of youth, and Baker uses two examples to illustrate the boomers' unrelenting search for it. Simultaneously watching *Seinfeld* on television and reading about "the new impotence pill," it occurs to him that both are about staying eternally young. But, he points out reasonably, "if young was meant to be the eternal human condition, medical science would not have invented liposuction. Or eye tucks." These and "all such medically engineered schemes for kidding yourself about the date of your first birthday" remind him of "something that Jonathan Swift is supposed to have said: 'Everybody wants to live forever, but nobody wants to grow old.'"[7]

Baker asks us to bear with him while he musters courage to speak of the impotence pill "in a publication of the sort that might once have been read at breakfast by my mother." He is, after all, "of that musty past when unhealthy repression of Utterly Tasteless Vulgarity made people recoil from talk of such stuff as impotence pills and semen-stained garments." The latter reference brings to mind Baker's column on the media's obsession with the unsavory details of the Bill-Monica affair, in which he wrote, "The Watergate journalists Woodward and Bernstein inspired a whole generation of young people to think of journalism as an honorable way to spend a life. That is the generation that's now trying to look solemn instead of leering and winking as it issues the daily bulletins on ladies' dirty linen."[8]

But in this column, instead of expressing his revulsion at all the publicity given to the impotence pill, Baker mentions it only in parenthesis—"(front-page newspaper play, lead story on network TV news)"—and then speculates, with mock alarm, on its unintended consequences for women:

> Can we doubt that millions of males will line up at pharmacies across the nation seeking libidinal enhancement? And that millions of these libidinally enhanced males will raise the sexual-harassment rate by a terrifying order of magnitude? Can the pharmaceutical world come up with a pill that women can take to repel the goatish advances of these pill-dosed males, many of whom will doubtless be old codgers eager to revisit spring, hence liable to fatal collapse if vigorously repelled? Surely the law will never hold women responsible for the deaths of these aged specimens. Still, the shock of being involved in a fatal encounter will be hard for many women to bear.

He then turns to *Seinfeld*, the sitcom whose enormous popularity made it a television phenomenon of the 1990s. Now that it was approaching the end of its run, explanations were being offered for its amazing success. Baker quotes one of them: "It was the perfect show for our age because it was about absolutely nothing." He disagrees with that explanation and, with ironic scorn worthy of the aforementioned Jonathan Swift, offers an explanation of his own:

> [T]he present age is not about absolutely nothing; it just seems that way. The present age is not about Utterly Tasteless Vulgarity either; that's just its idea of correct etiquette. What the present age is about is staying eternally young, and "Seinfeld" is the idea's fullest expression. Jerry and his

friends … are not just staying eternally young. They are doing something far more alluring to our age. They are refusing to grow up.

"'Seinfeld,'" Baker continues, "is the direct descendant of Mary Martin's glorious 'Peter Pan,' whose songs were bedtime lullabies forty years ago to the people who now run the country." He remembers "these people before they began to grow bald, before faint wrinkle lines appeared." He remembers them "in 'Peter Pan' singing out … 'I won't grow up! I won't grow up!' And here they are, forty years later, still faithful to the oath.…" There is a fondness in Baker's recollection that almost conceals his disgust.

"It Was a Very Good Year"

If Baker regarded the boomer generation with qualified affection, he viewed the generation that followed it with unmitigated delight. Taking his title from the tender, rueful ballad of a man now in the autumn of his life, Baker wrote a charming reminiscence of the six weeks that he and his wife spent as baby sitters for their thirteen-year-old granddaughter.

Bemused by her behavior and the behavior of her thirteen-year-old girlfriends, he reports his observations like an anthropologist writing about the members of a mysterious and intriguing tribe. A *fond* anthropologist: otherwise, he might have disapproved of the "luxuries America lavishes on its luckier young," such as the private telephone in his granddaughter's bedroom. It was always busy, too, and her friends had to phone the grandparents to interrupt her conversation. Which they did, every five minutes. "After a while one wanted to scream," Baker writes. "So did two, which is how many of us were on phone-answering duty."[9]

The private line had been justified as a tool that would let his granddaughter use her dial-up connection to the Internet without shutting down the general house phone. Baker wonders what she did on the Internet, because if they entered the room in which she was "toiling over it, she would … throw her body around the screen to block our view." She also had a private TV, which is why her private phone was busy even when the Internet was not connected. Baker explains the tribal ritual: "Two thirteen-year-old girls in different parts of town turn on the same

TV show.... Then they get on the phone to each other and keep the lines open discussing the show as it progresses."

Sometimes five or six thirteen-year-old girls came to the house and, after they left, Baker reports in a tone of perfect equanimity, "we would find spoons under the carpet, ice-cream-stained bowls in the fireplace, watermelon seeds under the sofa cushions." The grandparents complained with only the mildest of oaths because, Baker writes, the girls "reminded us of Proust. Those lovely summer girls of his at the seaside in Balbec—."

And when the six weeks ended, they "said sad farewells to … telephones, Internet, spoons under the carpet and the pain and beauty of being thirteen." The juxtaposition of pain and beauty suggests the poignant mixture of sadness and delight evoked in the aging man by the presence of "these lovely summer girls."

"Wish You Were Here"

"Wish You Were Here" is a portrait of New York by an artist in old age. Struck by the "breathtaking beauty of Manhattan in December" and wanting to write about it, Baker is dismayed to come up with nothing better than "the usual clichés: The evening light becomes 'magical.' Christmas lights in trees, windows and hotel lobbies 'sparkle like diamonds against the black velvet night.' There is much more that is worse," he admits. "I have thrown it in the trash."[10]

Baker thinks of F. Scott Fitzgerald, who wrote "wonderfully about the beauty of Manhattan," but then he reflects that "Fitzgerald's Manhattan evenings are glorious not only because his New York is a glorious city, but also because he sees it through eyes that are young and yearning, and not yet so hardened by experience that they look too closely for tinsel." Fitzgerald's "beautiful Manhattan was a summer place," he points out, where "under lavender skies of late afternoon he hurried down thrilling avenues to meet irresistible New York girls. I am of an age now to think of them as New York women," he adds, "but they are still irresistible, though not so irresistible in summer as in December."

"It is December that is New York's month for people of all ages," Baker writes at seventy-two. He returns to the subject of the Christmas lights, but this time he offers a realistic—and original—explanation of their magic. In this season, "night comes in midafternoon ... [and] the office towers blaze with light. A million windows lit in the city's gigantic file-cabinet towers work ... a miracle." By daylight these "overbearing office boxes are ... monstrous," but in a December mid-afternoon, when the lights must be turned on, "even the nightmarish architecture of Sixth Avenue becomes invisible."

Another magical effect of the lights is that they dispel the "subconscious sense of living in an oceanic city at the edge of the cold, gray, scary Atlantic, destroyer of Titanics." (Baker wrote this column fifteen years before the devastations of Hurricane Sandy changed his portentous sentence to a prescient one.) Against this background, "December lights make the city seem—strange word for New York—cosy.…

"New York is first and foremost a market town. Its primary business is selling. Its chief topic of conversation is money," Baker notes. Continuing the metaphor, he writes that "December is a month-long equivalent of market day in an old-fashioned county seat" and evokes the scene: "The streets are packed with modern versions of horses, wagons, carts and buggies. Double-parked trucks block narrow streets. Honking, bleating cars sit bumper to bumper, making a joyous noise ... and filling the air with oily grit." The percussive sounds and fast tempo of those sentences capture the frantic excitement of New York's streets in the Christmas season, and of its sidewalks, where "loaded shopping bags whack shins and thighs. Wheeled boxes smash into heels and tendons."

Baker returns to "the astonishing light that is Thomas Edison's gift to New York," which, with the "exciting busyness of crowded streets make the city feel as if a great festival is in progress. Indeed one is," he writes. "The city is celebrating the triumph of commerce." The satirist is not immune to "this ravishing December New York." He has seen "the beggars with their cardboard cups upheld" and he knows that "it is a tough town ... a terribly tough town," but also, in December, "I'll say it anyhow—magical."

Fitzgerald and Baker both wrote about the beauty of New York, one with the view of a young man captivated by the city's glamorous surfaces, the other with the view of a man who has lived long enough to see what is underneath them. The older writer's view doesn't contradict the younger writer's perception of beauty; it deepens it.

The New York Review of Books

Fitzgerald's famous observation that "there are no second acts in American lives" was proved wrong by Baker, who, after retiring from *The New York Times* in 1998, began a second career as a writer for *The New York Review of Books*. The editor, Robert Silvers, had begun his courtship of Baker in 1997, every now and then sending him a book with a "seductive note," wondering if Baker might be "interested in saying something about it." If Silvers "had asked for 'reviews,' none of these ... would have been written," Baker writes in his introduction to *Looking Back*, a selection of his pieces in the *New York Review*.[11]

He disliked book reviewing, which required "passing public judgment on the work of other writers" and "disposing" of a book that may have taken years to write "in a few hundred words, as the typical book review does...." But the word "review" was never spoken. "Instead," Baker tells us, "each book arrived, usually without warning, invariably accompanied by a brief note suggesting it might be such good reading that I just might end up wishing to write perhaps four thousand words about it." This was "a beguiling invitation" for someone who "had spent thirty-seven years writing a newspaper column two and a quarter inches wide and eighteen inches long." And since Baker was about to retire from the *Times* "after half a century in daily journalism," he was looking for "something new to do, preferably something entirely different" (xi).

But, he asked himself, after "years of writing constantly in this miniature form, ... was it still possible to learn something different?" It was a reasonable concern for a man in his mid-seventies but it was also typical of Baker's almost self-deprecating modesty. He had questioned his suitability for each promotion he was offered throughout his career in journalism: the evidence is in his memoir *The Good Times*.

As it turned out, the writing wasn't "entirely different." Baker's pieces, whether in *The New York Times* or *The New York Review*, were personal essays, the former based on his observations of contemporary American society, the latter on his readings of contemporary American books. The longer, more reflective form was suited to the longer view of the older writer and the storehouse of knowledge—of history, politics, journalism, literature, American culture, and human nature—acquired over a lifetime.

His reason for choosing certain books and sending others back unread was "age, mostly," Baker tells us. "I had begun to enjoy looking back more than one does in the summery years of life. The books that seemed most interesting were books that took me touring back into my own past" (xi). One such book was a biography of William Randolph Hearst, the newspaper tycoon who, besides introducing newspapers to Baker (as he had recalled in his farewell "Observer" column), had also provided Baker's first job in newspapers, "as a twelve-year-old entrepreneur running a two-block home-delivery route for his *Baltimore News-Post* and *Sunday American*." Opening Hearst's biography, Baker writes, "affected me as the madeleine affected Proust" (xii).

Baker also chose to write about books that took him back to his pre–"Observer" years, when he was a political reporter for the *Times*, and to four politicians he had spent "a lot of my working life keeping an eye on": Barry Goldwater, Richard Nixon, Lyndon Johnson, and Robert F. Kennedy (xiii–xiv). His "shameless bias toward elitism in journalism" drew Baker to the works of the great journalists Murray Kempton and Joseph Mitchell and to a "flurry of books looking back," produced by the seventy-fifth anniversary of *The New Yorker*. "Most of them," Baker notes, "sooner or later found the focus of their stories in William Shawn, the editorial maestro who had stayed on too long and been fired" (xv–xvi).

The gift for portraiture that had enlivened Baker's "Observer" columns with a cast of fictional characters and had brought to life the cast of real characters in his two memoirs, transformed a number of his essays in the *New York Review* into portraits of notable Americans. The three discussed here are portraits in old age of William Shawn, Robert Byrd, and Joseph Mitchell.

"The Love Boat"

"At the end when everything was crashing down around him William Shawn seems to have been an authentically tragic figure. Hundreds of artists and writers were prepared to attest to his nobility and did so frequently without being asked. He was nearly eighty years old when the fall came and had been editor of *The New Yorker* for thirty-five years."[12]

These opening sentences of "The Love Boat" introduce the two strands of Baker's story. It is a portrait of William Shawn in old age, when "the fall" from his exalted position as the great editor of a great magazine mirrored the trajectory of the hero of a Greek tragedy. It is also an examination of Shawn's relationships with *The New Yorker*'s artists and writers, who attested to his "nobility"—the requisite rank of a tragic hero—"frequently without being asked," a phrase that suggests their excessive eagerness to praise him. Drawing from a spate of books published or republished to coincide with the magazine's seventy-fifth birthday, Baker weaves the two strands into a tragicomedy.

He begins with James Thurber's book *The Years with Ross*, originally published in 1957, which, as its title makes clear, is about the years that Harold Ross, the magazine's founder and first editor, was in charge. In it, Thurber noted that, among "the good things [that] had happened to Ross in 1933, God sent him William Shawn," and that "without Shawn's hard work and constant counsel" as chief deputy editor, "Ross would never have made the distinguished record he did as editor during the war" (127–8).

From Thurber, "one of *The New Yorker*'s gods," who "with E. B. White helped create the distinctive *New Yorker* voice, this was high praise," observes Baker. "Not high enough, however, for Shawn's devotees, according to Ved Mehta, himself a Shawn admirer" (128). This leads Baker to Mehta's memoir *Remembering Mr. Shawn's New Yorker* (1998) and its description of a party at Shawn's apartment in the 1960s at which some *New Yorker* writers "were denigrating Thurber and his recently published book on Ross" (128). Shawn, "famous for shyness and dislike of confrontation seems to have been embarrassed by the incident and ended it graciously with a small lecture" on Thurber as one of the greatest humorists of the century and, Mehta wrote, under Shawn's "gentle prompting" everyone agreed (128–9).

What Baker finds striking about Mehta's account is "the sense it conveys of the group's devotion to Shawn. They may rage against those who deny him his due share of praise, but they quickly become calm and gentle as he subtly steers them toward a more generous, more civilized view of Thurber. He was an editor in complete control of a staff utterly devoted to him.... In later years," writes Baker, "this devotion came to be expressed by some of his admirers as 'love.' Many editors are admired," Baker says, "but there is something eerie about an editor being loved" (129).

That is because of the "cruel things" that editors do to writers' submissions. "Often they throw the work back into the submitter's face, declaring it unfit to print. Even when condescending to accept it they demand rewriting, restructuring, and slashing that often seems to turn the ... work into someone else's. It is unnatural to love someone who commits these cruelties on one's creative work," Baker declares, and he reminds us that "no editing matched *The New Yorker*'s for thoroughness" (129).

But not only did the writers not complain about Shawn's cruelties: they responded by writing of their love for him. In a satirical tone appropriate for the "Love Boat" theme (and for his view of Lillian Ross's tell-all memoir), Baker furnishes some examples:

> [H]ere are 414 pages by Mehta which amount to a declaration of love for Shawn—"the legendary, saintly, canonical Mr. Shawn" as Renata Adler calls him. And here is an astonishing memoir by Lillian Ross announcing for all the world to know that she loved Shawn and that Shawn loved her back with such vigor for so many years that she regarded herself as his wife. Hers is a love so overpowering that she must shout it out, regardless of any pain it might cause Shawn's wife and sons [129–30].

"Brendan Gill also loved Shawn," Baker continues, introducing the quintessential sophisticated *New Yorker* writer in a sentence he can't have written with a straight face (130). Gill's memoir *Here at the New Yorker*, originally published in 1975, was reissued with a new introduction in which Gill wrote that when Shawn "occasionally sent him a memo of thanks for performing some small favor and the memo ended 'With love,' then how grateful I had reason to be. For like everyone else on the magazine, I felt a desire, childish as it unquestionably was, to be a Shawn favorite, and even, still more childishly, to be first among his favorites."

This "bizarre confession," writes Baker, "brings to mind Proust's sleepless young Marcel yearning for *Maman* to come and kiss him good night" (130).

He returns to Renata Adler's memoir, *Gone*, in which she described her last visit to Shawn's office after he was fired. Baker's summary of her account of their tearful leave-taking and mutual avowals of love juxtaposes the tragic and comic aspects of his story:

> "First of all," she tells him, "it goes without saying, I love you and I hope to keep seeing you for the rest of our lives." Shawn interrupts, saying "'I love you' quite firmly." In their conversation they are "sometimes crying, sometimes not." Finally Adler rises, goes to the door to leave, and Shawn says, "in a tone of surprising firmness and, considering the distance, gentleness, 'I love you.' I said again that I loved him ..." [131].

Ben Yagoda's book *About Town* "best explains what made Shawn a superb editor," Baker writes (132). There was, first, "a capacity for taking infinite pains to achieve precision.... Out went every bit of 'extraneous, repetitive, or discordant material' and in their place Shawn inserted 'just the right word, phrase, or sentence.... Almost invariably [the writers] conceded that Shawn's editing had improved their work without changing its content.'" Yagoda suggested that Shawn "'got away with his aggressions because the staff could not but respond to his profound attention, strong respect for, and unabashed flattery of their work.'" Baker sums it up: "He loved them, and they loved him back" (133).

And yet, "not every writer was so enchanted by a Shawn editing," Baker says, and again quotes Vad Mehta, who, in spite of all his praise for Shawn, complained that "now that I was at *The New Yorker* I seemed to be incapable of writing even a letter off the top of my head" (133). Baker wonders if a reason for the waning productivity of some of the *New Yorker* writers was Shawn's perfectionism, no matter how tactfully expressed. Or not expressed. Shawn often bought a piece and "put it in deep storage with dozens of other pieces destined never to reach the newsstands because [he] didn't think them good enough but hated to tell their authors" (133).

The staff called him "Mr. Shawn," which showed extraordinary respect "in a publishing world where the most august figures were called simply by nicknames or ungarnished last names," Baker writes, adding mischievously that "only Lillian Ross calls him 'Bill,' thus asserting her primacy on the love ladder" (131). He doubts that Shawn encouraged "the Mistering," but, Baker points out, "the old-fashioned politeness of it spoke of something he was trying to preserve in the magazine.... It declared that civility and politeness still mattered at *The New Yorker*" (131). This was "a daring attitude to strike after the 1960s," he writes, "when civility and politeness came to be viewed ... as quaint remnants of a reactionary generation whose time had passed. Shawn and his *New Yorker* were struggling against a tide that threatened to sweep civility and politeness out of American life. In his old age he was to pay dearly for it" (132).

One example of that "old-fashioned politeness" was Shawn's refusal to print "he-man prose" in *The New Yorker*, a policy that had begun with Harold Ross (136). Baker, while sympathetic to Shawn, points out that "even in the 1980s, when custom and the Supreme Court had authorized wholesale use of what Ross once called 'daring words,' Shawn refused to allow them in the magazine" (135). There were adverse reactions to this policy: "Younger writers complained that it showed *The New Yorker* was no longer in the cultural mainstream. Marketers worried about declining ad revenue and circulation argued that the policy made the magazine seem too old-fashioned to interest young consumers" (136).

The hero in Greek tragedy is brought down by his fatal flaw of hubris. Perhaps Shawn's hubris was that he believed himself irreplaceable and when that belief extended into his old age, it was manifested in his resistance to naming a successor. In Renata Adler's view, writes Baker, Shawn never had any intention of permitting the magazine to survive him. "Splendid though he had been, her Mr. Shawn had begun to lose his grip.... He was approaching eighty and should have known that octogenarians cannot go on and on. If he didn't then it was surely time for him to step aside" (136).

And when he didn't step aside, they fired him. In 1984, *The New Yorker* was sold to a publishing conglomerate, whose head, S. I. Newhouse, agreed to let Shawn stay on to pick a successor. Three years later, when it was clear that Shawn would never voluntarily part from the magazine, Newhouse appointed Robert Gottlieb, then the chief editor at Knopf, to Shawn's position. Again drawing on the words in the books by *New Yorker* writers who were present, Baker re-creates the "last sadly comic act ... played out in *The New Yorker* offices the day that Shawn received his pink slip" (137).

Adler's description of Shawn at this stage, writes Baker, "suggests a tragic Lear-like figure, a dithering old man, once master of his world, now shocked when Newhouse, in 1987, fires him" (137). The members of the staff gathered to express their own shock and their devotion to Shawn, and to take action, which, as Baker says, "these being writers, meant composing a letter" to send to Gottlieb, urging him not to accept the job. According to Ben Yagoda, the letter was signed by 153 people, and, Baker tells us, "Gottlieb, of course, took the job anyway" (138).

He concludes the story with an excerpt from Shawn's farewell letter to his staff. "His letter spoke of love," Baker writes in an ironic but touching understatement for a letter that began, "We have built something quite wonderful together. Love has been the controlling emotion, and love is the essential word" and that ended, "I must speak of love once more. I love all of you, and will love you as long as I live" (138).

Then, in a brief, respectful summation, Baker writes of Shawn, "He lived to be eighty-five. In the vital years of his manhood he had cherished his dignity and his privacy." He saves his irony for Shawn's staff: "After his death, those who claimed to love him seem to have thought his dignity and privacy no longer mattered. They began to write books" (138).

"Troublemaker"

The publication of the book *Losing America*, written by Robert Byrd when he was eighty-five years old and had been a member of the U.S. Senate for forty-five years, was the occasion of Baker's candid and lively portrait of the senator in old age. Drawing on his own experience as a political reporter who had covered the White House and the Senate for the *Times* and on his considerable knowledge of American history, Baker also gives us an intimate and informed picture of the Senate, where Byrd's portrait is set.

"Robert Byrd, Democrat of West Virginia learned how to be a United States senator under the tutelage of serious men," Baker begins. Readers familiar with Baker's style are quite sure that "serious men" is an ironic phrase that will lead to a serious point.[13] "Committees were run by shrewd old tyrants who had been senators almost forever," he continues. "Mostly Southerners and deeply racist, these chairmen were still perpetuating segregation nearly a century after Appomattox.... Most of the grandees were Democrats, for Democrats had been in the majority for most of the previous thirty years. So long accustomed to power, they had become arrogant in its uses." Baker furnishes several personally witnessed examples of past senators behaving badly to illustrate, he says, that "in those years, a senator was somebody."

Then he makes his serious point: "A senator of that era who too flagrantly played political lackey to the president had to endure the contempt of his colleagues. The Senate—by God and by Madison!—was not created to mouth lines scripted by the White House's paid hacks. The Senate was created to prevent presidents from governing recklessly and to bring them to their senses when they persisted in governing recklessly anyhow.

"The awkward truth, of course," Baker writes, "is that the Senate in which Robert Byrd learned the ropes was utterly and complacently undemocratic, just as the founders designed it to be. The constitutional design is still unchanged: six-year terms still insulate the members of the Senate against the political passions which bedevil presidents and House members; with each state limited to two votes regardless of size, small and sparsely settled states still enjoy lopsided power over the teeming masses."

What changed was the character of the Senate and it changed "alarmingly," Byrd wrote in *Losing America*. The change enabled the "rogue White House," as Byrd called the administration of George W. Bush, "to get away with a broad assault on the Constitution.... While traditional American liberties, as well as the constitutional powers of Congress were being overridden by the Bush circle, Congress chooses to just salute the emperor and then stand down."

Byrd was referring to Congress's granting the President a free hand to make war in Iraq. "Byrd disapproves of the war, and almost everything else about the Bush administration, including the character and behavior of the President himself," Baker writes. Acknowledging that "many Democrats have become disapprovers since Bush's popularity polls began sinking," he points out that "Byrd disapproved back when the false alarms about 'weapons of mass destruction' had hard-headed politicians wishing the President godspeed to Bagdad...."

"That the House of Representatives bowed so readily to the President is not surprising," Baker says, explaining that because "all 435 members may, in theory, be voted out of office every two years, the House is easily stampeded during big political storms." But the "surrender" of the Senate was something new. With a party discipline of "Teutonic severity," even the Senate, "with its traditional hospitality to mavericks, malcontents, self-servers, and rascals, has found its Republicans submissive to the beat of the White House drummer." As a result, "instead of moderating the House's natural enthusiasm for radical responses to September 11, the Senate has trooped obediently along behind it."

Returning to Byrd's *Losing America*, Baker writes that "the senate's readiness to fall supine before the White House pains Byrd almost as much as George Bush angers him and the result is a highly intemperate book." This delights Baker and he introduces the book and its author in an exuberant passage that celebrates the freedom granted by old age to speak one's mind. (Byrd's book is the embodiment of the point that Baker made in his "Observer" column "Don't Believe It, Kids"):

> Eighty-six years old, fifty-one years a member of Congress, a former Democratic leader of the Senate, former chairman of the Senate Appropriations Committee, Byrd flails away at Bush and his docile Congress with the zeal of a campus radical.... Byrd has discovered—in the nick of time—that very old age, however heavy its hardships, can also leave one free at last. How sweet it must be for a politician, after half a century of holding his tongue, to speak his mind as Byrd does in appraising the President.

"Coming from a liberal, this rough judgment on Bush would hardly be news," Baker writes, "but during his half-century in Congress no one ever accused Byrd of being a liberal." He lists Byrd's attributes as a senator without comment, while making clear Byrd's record as an opportunist ("a practical fellow") and a racist:

> When new to the Capitol he obviously absorbed Speaker Sam Rayburn's famous advice to newcomers: "If you want to get along, go along." Byrd was a go-along man. He was a hawk on Vietnam. He declined to battle for civil rights. Byrd was a practical fellow, and the Southerners who

could make or break a new man's career had no use for "do-gooders" and "bleeding hearts" agitating for the right of black Americans. For a brief period Byrd was a member of the Ku Klux Klan.

Baker finds it "revealing" that Byrd "faults Bush for not paying his dues. Byrd surely paid his," he writes. And, again without comment, he summarizes Byrd's bootstrap climb from poverty to politics. A refrain that pervades Baker's coming-of-age memoir, *Growing Up*, is his mother's repeated urging to "make something of yourself," a value that she instilled in him. One assumes that Baker must have admired this quality in Byrd.

> Orphaned at the age of one and brought up by an aunt and uncle, he pulled himself up out of bleakest poverty in the Appalachian coal fields; worked as a gas pumper, meat cutter, and shipyard welder; studied at a variety of small West Virginia colleges; got elected to the state legislature and then in 1952 to Congress where he spent the next fifty years building a conservative Democratic record.

When Byrd arrived in the Senate, Lyndon Johnson put him on the Appropriations Committee and by 1989 he had become its Chairman, "a job," Baker points out, "that licenses its holders to pillage the federal treasury for the benefit of the good, needy folks back home. West Virginia always had a disproportionate number of needy folks, and Byrd became famous in Washington for directing federal boons their way." And yet, he shows some sympathy for Byrd, who was snubbed by many of his colleagues, although Baker's sympathy for Byrd is prompted, and eclipsed, by his contempt for the new breed of rich, media-hungry senators:

> Because his hand was on the federal purse, Byrd was an important figure but not really top-drawer or A-list dinner material, not in a class with the headline makers, stuffed with unrevealable classified dope and byzantine circumlocution, who performed on the weekend TV talk shows. In a Senate rapidly turning into a millionaires' club, he remained old-fashioned, countrified, slightly out of place in the modern age.

After Byrd entered Congress, he spent ten years getting his law degree in night school and, for the first time, Baker shows his admiration for the senator who "read history with the passion of a man discovering late in life that his own age owes large debts to the past." The recognition of the debts owed by the living to the past is an important matter for Baker. In his memoir *The Good Times*, he described burying his mother in the Virginia churchyard where Baker's father and generations of his father's family were buried, and noted that "a burying ground is a good place to remind the living that they have debts to the past."[14]

In Byrd's "occasional tutorials on the floor," as Baker refers with polite irony to the speeches of the famously longwinded senator, he "reminded the members that the Roman Senate's surrender to dictatorial strong men had led to the fall of the Roman republic." He quotes from Byrd's earlier book, *The Senate of the Roman Republic*, in which he had written that it was "the progressive decline of the already supine [Roman] Senate that led to the end of the republic." And, adds Baker, "that it could also happen here is the message of *Losing America*."

"Parallels between Rome and modern Washington can be pushed only so far before turning silly," he acknowledges, "but it is worth noting what great Julius planned to do next after he saw the Senate becoming surly about his dictatorial ways: he started planning a Middle East war against the Parthians." Citing this parallel between Caesar's and Bush's wars in the Middle East also gives Baker the opportunity to inform us that "the Parthians were a tribe of tireless troublemakers," which, in turn, leads to his name for the new role that the former go-along senator assumed late in his career.

"That Byrd was becoming a troublemaker," writes Baker, "went generally unnoticed until the White House asked Congress to license a presidential war in Iraq. Until then the only discontent stirring in the Senate came from an ineffectual minority composed of the usual suspects: Ted Kennedy, a handful of Democratic liberals, and, of course, John McCain, the supreme Republican sorehead who still seemed cross about the royal smearing the Bush people had given him in South Carolina's 2000 presidential primary."

In the fall of 2002, the Bush-Cheney administration asked for a congressional resolution—a method of going to war, Baker reminds us, that was "pioneered by Lyndon Johnson with the Tonkin Gulf resolution of 1964" and led to the war in Vietnam. Many of Byrd's colleagues regretted having voted for LBJ's resolution and "swore they would never vote for such an abomination again. But," asks Baker, his scorn equally directed at the senators and the times, "how can a busy senator here in this frantic multitasking age be expected to study the past? They were doomed to repeat it."

Byrd, however, remembered the past. "We had handed off too much to Lyndon Johnson with the Gulf of Tonkin Resolution," he wrote in *Losing America*. "Did no one remember that, and its tragic aftermath?" He argued for a delay in order to slow down the process, but "with elections imminent," Baker writes, "Democrats found it safer to give the President what he wanted." And what he wanted was "virtually unlimited authority to make preemptive war on Iraq." With caustic clarity, Baker summarizes Byrd's account of the administration's "war salesmanship," which culminated in the resolution that Byrd called "a complete handing over of congressional war power to the president."

Byrd was outraged: "What would the framers have thought? In this terrible show of weakness, the Senate left an indelible stain upon its own escutcheon." Baker tells us that, "before the shooting started, Byrd had become a familiar figure to C-SPAN addicts by frequently questioning Bush's policies on the Senate floor." As his speeches gained wider notice, Byrd became the butt of a certain amount of name-calling, which included the predictable epithets "traitor" and "KKK," along with ageist taunts of "senile" and "old man." But only the old man dared to speak the truth about the emperor's new clothes.

Baker concludes his piece with Byrd's "entertaining sketch of himself brought to high dudgeon by the President's cavalier executive style." The occasion was a gathering of congressional leaders, summoned by Bush to the White House to learn about a bill to establish the Department of Homeland Security. The bill had been written by members of the White House staff, secretly and without input from Congress, and Bush wanted Congress—which was about to leave for its annual August vacation—to pass it in time for the first anniversary of September 11.

Byrd described the meeting as a public relations event staged for television, during which Bush offered "desultory" remarks about creating a new department and thanked Congress for its advice and cooperation. When it was over and Bush announced that he was leaving, Byrd asked for permission to speak. Baker quotes an excerpt from Byrd's account of what he said to the President, the President's response, and Byrd's opinion of the latter: "It was obvious that he had no idea what was in his Department of Homeland Security proposal, nor did he seem to care."

Baker reminds us of the unique credential that Byrd brought to his evaluation of President Bush: his unparalleled longevity as a senator. "Byrd had sat in meetings with presidents since Harry Truman," Baker writes, and then he lets the senator have the last word: "But this president, this Bush number 43, was in a class by himself—ineptitude supreme. This meeting with Bush the Younger topped anything I had seen, from Truman on, for absolute tripe!"

"Out of Step with the World"

Baker's essay-review of Joseph Mitchell's books is a sympathetic and sensitive portrait of Mitchell in old age. It is also a portrait of Mitchell's New York, which, Baker writes, "is long vanished." He isn't sure whose New York has succeeded it, but "Tom Wolfe's, painted in his broad, gaudy, burlesque strokes would have to be considered."[15]

Referring to a scene in Wolfe's novel *The Bonfire of the Vanities*, in which a character dies "while dining in a fancy East Side restaurant ... [and] the management's only concerns are to get the body out fast and to collect the bill for the dead man's unfinished meal," Baker notes that "some readers thought Wolfe unjustly cruel to the city, and maybe he was. Still, in the present New York," he writes in 2001, "people go out to dinner, pay a thousand dollars a bottle for the wine, and go home to three-million-dollar apartments while others are bedding down on sidewalks in cardboard boxes. Only burlesque can catch the spirit of it" (173).

He reflects that "New Yorks come and go so quickly that literature has trouble keeping up with them. From Washington Irving to Poe to Melville to Whitman to Edith Wharton, somebody's 'old New York' has always been turning into a new city. Joseph Mitchell became its chronicler as F. Scott Fitzgerald was leaving the scene, and Mitchell's city would have absolutely none of the gauzy romantic charm of Fitzgerald's" (173–4).

Mitchell arrived in New York on October 25, 1929, the day after the stock market crashed. Besides comparing Wolfe and Mitchell as voices of their respective New Yorks, Baker points out that, despite writing about New York in a "dark time," Mitchell also saw and conveyed its "sweetness of character which eased the hard lives he recorded" (174). And without directly judging Wolfe's novel, Baker suggests that it shared the vulgarity and grossness of its subject.

Mitchell was a chronicler of the Bowery, Times Square, the waterfront, the fish market, and workingmen's saloons, and "through the middle third of the twentieth century he ... created a tapestry of New York lives comparable to Charles Dickens's astonishing assortment of Victorian Londoners." Like Dickens, Mitchell "roamed his city looking for people worth preserving in stories" and, Baker writes, "just as Dickens's fictional Londoners seem more real than life, Mitchell's real New Yorkers seem born to live in novels" (174–5).

Both Dickens and Mitchell began as reporters and, as a former reporter himself, Baker notes that Dickens's "inability to keep his passions out of his writing may have helped make him a great novelist, but it made for some very bad journalism," while Mitchell "was trained in the hard discipline of an old-fashioned journalism, whose code demanded self-effacement of the writer." Baker makes an interesting comparison between the discipline by which Mitchell worked and "the artistry needed to compose good music: the writer had to stir an emotional or intellectual response in his audience without telling them how to feel or think," and he suggests that Mitchell's portraits of people "are worth close study by writers who want to learn how to move an audience without preaching a lesson."

They usually start as if they are going to be funny, "then almost deliberately deceive this expectation and become touching and sometimes terribly sad, as in 'Lady Olga'" (176–7). "Lady Olga" was Jane Barnell, a sixty-nine-year-old woman whose life had been spent as a "bearded lady" in circus sideshows. After identifying her by her stage name, Baker refers to her thereafter as "Miss Barnell," perhaps out of respect and perhaps to emphasize that Mitchell did not dwell on her freakishness. He was "out to explore what it means to be a 'freak' in America," writes Baker, "and the notion that we are going to be titillated with anecdotes about Miss Barnell's bizarre appearance vanishes as he piles up details. What emerges is a portrait of a woman who has spent most of her life in pain" (177).

The people Mitchell liked to write about, first as a young reporter at the New York *Herald-Tribune* and later in his *New Yorker* profiles—people like Jane Barnell and Florence Cubitt ("Tanya, Queen of the Nudists") and "Cockeye Johnny" and others whom Baker brings to life a second time in his own mini-portraits of them—were said to be "eccentrics," people who were "sadly or humorously out of step with the world," as Brendan Gill put it (177). Since Baker drew from Gill's description for his title (or it was chosen by the editor after reading Baker's piece), presumably he was suggesting that Mitchell himself, in old age, was out of step with the world (179).

"His New York was born of the crash, hardened by the Great Depression, civilized by the sense of mission generated by World War II, and made genial by the Eisenhower era's sense of well-being," Baker writes. "When he stopped writing in the 1960s, the inevitable change was almost complete" (174). Baker describes that change in a satirical and evocative paragraph that reminds us that he too was a chronicler of life in America, including New York, and that he had located the beginning of that change in the 1960s:

> The martini hour was ending; marijuana, hallucinogens, and the needle in the arm were the new way. The tinkling piano in the next apartment was giving way to the guitar in the park. People now had so much money that they could afford to look poor.... College students, who had once rioted for the pure joy of it, began rioting for moral and political uplift, issued non-negotiable demands, held the dean hostage, and blew up the physics lab. Gangster funerals disappeared into the back of newspapers, upstaged by spectacular nationally televised funerals of murdered statesmen [174].

Mitchell, who died in 1996 at the age of eighty-eight, wrote almost nothing during the last thirty years of his life. "He did not announce that he was going out of business or retire to enjoy rustic solitude," writes Baker. "He did not clean out his desk while mourning colleagues watched. He did not even stop coming to the office" at *The New Yorker* (182). "It worried people that he quit writing," Baker says, and adds, rather sharply, that "American writers are conditioned by the nation's market culture to suppose that no amount of success can explain why a writer sound of mind and body should cease production after thirty or forty years of what, for most writers, at least, is an extremely exacting and decidedly lonely line of work" (183).

"The fancies of Mitchell's colleagues tended toward the idea of 'writer's block,'" Baker continues, his tone becoming sardonic when he defines writer's block as "a disease especially widespread among college students, which leaves its victim's writing faculties in a state of paralysis, rendering him powerless to put words on paper for fear they may reveal he is not yet Shakespeare's equal" (183). He points out that "since it is a disease of egocentrics (also of people who want to be famous writers, but don't much like to write), Mitchell would have been immune; as a reporter he always left his ego at home when he went to work" (183). This is a tribute to Mitchell and to the profession of journalism. Writing was their job: the finished piece was the result of hard work, not of waiting for inspiration.

"As for paralysis," writes Baker, "there is evidence that in his eighties he could write as gracefully as he wrote at forty and fifty" (185). When *Up in the Old Hotel*, a collection of his *New Yorker* profiles, was published in 1992, Mitchell, who was then eighty-four, contributed an "Author's Note" that "was remarkable for the beauty with which it evoked a sense of his childhood. Never before had he written so intimately about himself," Baker tells us (183). "And he wrote of summer Sundays in a southern childhood" (184).

Mitchell was born in 1908 into a North Carolina farm family that "had grown cotton, tobacco, corn, and timber in that part of the world since before the Revolutionary War," Baker writes. "As in a lot of the rural South, families there commonly buried the dead in their farm fields, creating small private cemeteries shaded by groves of cedar or magnolia and enclosed by cast-iron fences. Generations of Mitchell kin were scattered among these small burying grounds, and they were not allowed to be forgotten quickly" (184).

Then, drawing from Mitchell's "Author's Note," and his own imagination, Baker evokes one of those summer Sundays of Mitchell's childhood:

> Summertime brought a traditional family watermelon-cutting ceremony in a picnic grove behind an old church his mother's ancestors had

helped build. When the melons were eaten and family talk was winding down and the afternoon was getting late, his Aunt Annie would lead a procession into the cemetery talking about the past, now and then pausing at a grave to "tell us about the man or woman down below..." [184–5].

This scene at Mitchell's family cemetery again brings to mind the end of Baker's memoir *The Good Times*, when he writes of burying his mother in the Virginia churchyard. "Never get me back up there in those sticks," his mother had said when they left their home in rural Virginia in 1930 after Baker's father died. Baker explained why he had taken her back to "those sticks" in this sentence (whose final phrase I quoted in "Troublemaker"):

> Burying her there was done out of a sense that a family is many generations closely woven; that though generations die, they endure as part of the fabric of the family; and that a burying ground is a good place to remind the living that they have debts to the past.[16]

Baker tells us that, looking back at his work in old age, Mitchell wrote that he was "surprised" and "pleased" to find it filled with what he thought was "graveyard humor" because "graveyard humor is an exemplification of the way I look at the world." It didn't seem odd to Baker that Mitchell stopped writing when he did. "He had done it for a very long time," Baker writes, "and though he had been terribly good at what he did, after a while one must lose his zest for doing it again and again" (185).

What *did* seem odd to Baker was that "a man with the memory of those Carolina Sundays in his bones should have found the New York of the middle third of the twentieth century the ideal subject for his civilized form of graveyard humor. The New York emerging in the 1960s ... needed writers who had grown up hearing the roar of the bullhorn, not the voice of Aunt Annie talking about the people down below" (185).

It doesn't seem odd to me that Baker, a man with the memory of those Virginia summers in his bones, should have found the New York—and the America—of the last half of the twentieth century the ideal subject for the trenchant and elegant satire that is *his* civilized form of graveyard humor.

10

Interview with Russell Baker

In the late 1990s Russell Baker and his wife, Mimi, left New York City and moved to the small town of Leesburg, Virginia. Located forty miles northwest of Washington, D.C., Leesburg is a historic town: It has been the Loudon county seat since 1758 and both armies traveled through it during the Civil War. Leesburg figures in Baker's personal history too. It is near Morrisonville, Virginia, the village in Northern Virginia where Baker was born in 1925 and where his parents and past generations of Bakers are buried.

On October 21, 2006, I took a taxi from the D.C. airport to Leesburg. Tucked away on a corner of Market Street, Leesburg's main thoroughfare, and hidden by the neighboring commercial buildings, the house was barely visible from the window of the cab. But up close, the house looked large and long, and as Baker, who greeted me at the front door, pointed out, it was actually three houses joined together. This was the handiwork of the Bakers' son Michael, who had restored each of the three sections to the style of its original period—with the sensible exception of two identical kitchens, which were designed for modern convenience. The ceilings, constructed for a shorter generation, were too low for Baker, who is over six feet tall and who ducked slightly whenever he crossed the threshold of a room.

The garden was also large and long. Walking its length of three-quarters of a mile and back again provided Baker's daily exercise. It looked like an English garden with its profusion of flowers and trees—although on this late October day only one crab apple tree was in bloom—and little vistas that provided views of them from different angles. Baker looked rather English too, I thought, in his white knitted cardigan as he guided me over the rustic terrain.

The interview took place in Baker's study, which, like all the other rooms in the two-story house, was warm and inviting

10—Interview with Russell Baker

> *and impeccably neat. Also impeccably neat were the complete files of the "Observer" that Baker keeps in slender black binders, carefully catalogued and dated. He showed me his first year's "Observer" columns from 1962, the earliest of them without a byline. Baker writes on a computer now—there were three of them in the study—after all those years of using a typewriter, the once-legendary tool of the journalist.*

Esther Harriott: In your memoir Growing Up **you show what it was like to grow up during the hardships of the Depression, but you also show the richness and strength provided by living with the members of an extended family, all under one roof. Have certain ways of looking at the world stayed with you from those days?**

Russell Baker: Mostly, I would think, the sense of the importance of family, of close family ties. Given the choice between family and state, I would pick the family, because during the Depression it proved to be the basic survival unit. I still feel that way about my own family—we're extremely close. That experience in the thirties of living with all those people in the house, relatives down on their luck, was kind of a good time, in a strange way, for a child.

Harriott: Did your early experience of poverty affect your attitudes about money throughout your life? Some people raised during the Depression seem to have a lifelong fear of spending money, even if they've become affluent.

Baker: Oh yeah, I have that. I still bend over when I see a penny on the sidewalk and pick it up. [*Laughs*] That's one percent interest on a dollar, more than the bank pays in my checking account.

Harriott: The central role that your mother played in your development as a person and as a writer dominates the memoir. But the powerful chapter you wrote about your father's death when you were five suggests that his death played an important role in your development too. I'm thinking especially of that devastating last paragraph. [Reads]: After that I never cried again with any real conviction, nor expected much of anyone's God except indifference, nor loved deeply without fear that it would cost me dearly in pain. At the age of five I had become

a skeptic, and began to sense that any happiness that came my way might be the prelude to some grim cosmic joke.

I remember writing that. It's one of the few places in the book where I stepped out of the character of the kid and spoke from the point of view of the man, at whatever age I then was.

It's all the more powerful because it is separate from the rest, both in tone and in being printed as a brief paragraph that stands on its own. Did you continue to feel that way?

A paper written by a student at a theological school compared the memoir to the Book of Job. I didn't get the comparison [*laughs*] but it was an interesting paper—how Job went through all those terrible trials and, in the end, maintained his loyalty to God and his equanimity.

Looking at your life from the outside, it certainly doesn't remind me of Job's. In your career, for example, success came very early and it lasted. You won a Pulitzer Prize for your "Observer" columns and another Pulitzer for Growing Up, *which was also a best seller. You are widely read and I would say loved. But that paragraph about your reaction to your father's death suggests that your enjoyment of success was tainted by that early blow.*

Yeah, it warped my mind. I've always been reluctant to have a good time because if the "old fella" thinks I'm having too good a time, he's going to punish me for it. And I've been reluctant to celebrate any success.

Do you attribute your attitude entirely to the trauma of your father's death? Couldn't there have been other things that shaped your thinking that way—your formidable grandmother, for instance?

My grandmother was an authoritarian figure, but she was loving.

Yes, and you certainly show that in your memoir. What I meant was that, because of her puritanical outlook, she may have conveyed the feeling that one should always be mindful of the possibility of downfall.

I think that's something very old in the American character, really. The founders worried about man's sinfulness and inadequacy. That's why the Constitution tries to guard against it.

Your second memoir, **The Good Times,** *was also very well received.*
Yeah, although there's a lot in that book that I felt was boring.

It isn't boring! It's fun to read.
Well, some of it was fun to write, but a lot of it was dull. I didn't want to write so much about my political reporting. But I felt that in this kind of book, I had to. So I did, and it was heavy going.

The section that's especially delicious is when you were sent to London by the **Baltimore Sun**—*a low-paid young reporter suddenly catapulted into the lap of luxury and English high society. And the hilarious story about your walking to the coronation of Queen Elizabeth in top hat and tails, carrying your lunch in a brown paper bag.*
[*Laughs*] A kid in London. That was a rare, delightful experience—the whole thing.

I've always thought that the voice in your writing was distinctively yours. But in your preface to one of the collections of your "Observer" columns, you wrote that you changed your voice for different columns, depending on the subject of the column. Would you explain that?
You have to change the voice constantly. If you used the same voice every day, people would get bored. So it might be foxy grandpa or the font of wisdom or Mr. Inside Information. Now that I'm long out of journalism, I find that I read fewer and fewer columns because it's the same thing over and over.

I miss humor in columns now, too. Gerald Nachman wrote an essay called "Whatever Became of Russell Baker or Who Killed the Humor Column?" and his point was that a great journalistic tradition, the comic essay, is nearly extinct. He said that newspapers had produced America's legendary humorists, Twain and Mencken.
And Art Buchwald.

Yes, in fact he wrote about the loss of "the four invincible B's"—Baker, Buchwald, [Dave] Barry, and [Irma] Bombeck. And, as an example of what has replaced them, he cited Maureen Dowd's columns in the Times, *which he said were full of clever wisecracks about politicians, but no humorous observations about society.*
The nature of journalism has changed and that might be part of it.

There's a lot of humor on television now. Every kid in the country watches Jon Stewart. I watch Jon Stewart myself. He's funny and very acute politically.

This is a question about age—your age—and I won't ask you to answer it if you prefer not to. Gerald Nachman also referred to your "forced, unhappy departure from the New York Times." I wondered if that was true and, if so, was it because the Times wanted a younger voice?

It wasn't unhappy for me. I talked to Arthur Sulzberger, young Arthur, who was by then the publisher. We had a pretty good relationship—I always found it easy to talk to him. I had begun to feel that I was too old for what I was doing, I had done it for too long, and it was time to change my life.

Change your life?

Well, do another kind of work. Doing this column week after week, year after year, I had begun to feel I was on what Fred Allen called a treadmill to oblivion. And it wasn't going anywhere.

Except that it was so good. There was never a drop in quality or interest.

I want to quash the idea that it was an unhappy thing for me. I had been talking about giving it up for some time. Generations had come and gone while I was doing the column. I'd come into the office in New York and I didn't know anybody. It looked like they were right out of high school, these people. I could see that they were looking at me and I wondered what they were thinking. "Who is this old guy and what is he doing here?" I'd begun to feel that, and I did feel that Arthur had taken over and naturally had his own ideas for the paper. And then one day he suggested cutting back. We did it in stages.

I remember when you stopped writing the Sunday Observer.

Baker: Oh, I insisted on that. That was my decision, entirely. I'm talking about the daily "Observer," which was twice a week. He suggested that they put me on contract and go to one a week, which was all I was doing at the end. So it was a gradual easing out. It was a good way to do it. And there was no unhappiness on my part, no sense of pressure.

So that was a misapprehension of Gerald Nachman's?

Yeah. There were some pieces written at the time, suggesting that

Sulzberger had leaned on me, but that wasn't true. It was a mutual decision.

And then you did change your life by becoming the host of the television series, Masterpiece Theatre. Was it difficult to make the transition from writing the column to writing introductions and conclusions?

Yeah, it was. It's another kind of writing, entirely. I'd say the main difference between television and the written page is that people don't care what you're saying, they care how you look. Their first comment is going to be about how you looked on television. You looked funny! You looked unhappy! You wore a funny necktie! I had trouble controlling my hands and everybody noticed that my hands were flying around. So that's the first thing. The second thing is that the introductions are really extremely short, much shorter than anything I'd ever written before. If I'd done an introduction of column-length for television, it would have taken me five minutes to give it. And they didn't have five minutes on television.

How long did it take you to write them? I know it's usually harder to write short than to write long.

Yeah, it takes a lot of time to write short. I had a terrible time at first. It took me a while to learn how to write for television. I think it's a special art and it's hard to learn. There are tricks, and the first one is that you can't use polysyllabic words—for example, you don't want to try to say "polysyllabic." You avoid words that are hard to pronounce clearly. You always look for a shorter word. So everything tends to be very brief. It's a kind of Anglo-Saxon speech.

You like that though, don't you? I mean, you avoid Latinate prose in all your writing.

Words with Latin roots, yeah, although sometimes they're essential. But mostly it's a matter of making the words easy to say because if you stumble you've got to stop and shoot the thing all over again.

Then, after making the transition from writing for print to writing for television, you made the transition from writing short to writing long, in your 4,000-word essay-reviews for The New York Review of Books.

And you've written a lot of these—they've been appearing every few issues.

Yeah, Silvers [the editor] likes them.

And why not!

The last one I did was about Andrew Mellon and I no sooner finished it than Silvers sent me a huge biography of Andrew Carnegie. And I bounced it back. Stop! I'm tired of rich Scots named Andrew! Anyway, Carnegie was a rather dull guy. I liked Mellon. I mean, he fascinated me.

And you wrote a fascinating portrait of him. You've always written about people—real people in your memoirs and imaginary ones in your Observer columns. And now you're writing about the authors or the people in their books. Your review of Losing America *by Senator Robert Byrd book was really a warts-and-all portrait of Byrd. And it actually made him a sympathetic figure.*

Poor Byrd. He was one of the few guys making sense of why the war in Iraq was a bad idea, why it was a *terrible* idea. And nobody paid any attention to him. "Oh, he's that quavery old guy from West Virginia." And Byrd was giving them home truths. Not a nice man, though. It's always the bastards you have to look to for guidance, unfortunately.

I found your review of Joseph Mitchell's reissued books—which were collections of his portraits of people—very moving, especially the story of how, for the last thirty years of his life, he kept going to his office at the New Yorker *every day but didn't write a word.*

I never quite solved the mystery of Joe Mitchell. I once met him. I sat with him through a dinner at the Academy of Arts and Letters and he was a fascinating guy. Very old by that time, but he had all these memories. He reminisced about Stanley Walker, the great city editor of the *New York Herald Tribune*, and all sorts of interesting people. Good talker, bright, witty.

But he couldn't put it down on paper any more?

He hadn't written anything for years. I always suspected that Shawn [*William Shawn, editor of* The New Yorker] didn't get on his back and make him write. Because he could have gone on writing. The man I had dinner with that night could certainly write as well as I could, if not better, and he had a fund of stories. So why didn't he? Well, part of it might be that he had so much money that he didn't have to write any more.

Maybe he just got tired of writing. That hasn't happened to you, has it?

Well, I'm tired of writing what I *was* writing. People said, "Oh, don't you miss the column?" I'd never want to write another column. There were times in the past year or so that I'd find myself thinking, oh, I wish I had the column these days. There's so much to be said that nobody's touched on. But I didn't really want to do that any more. I've done that. Let's go to the next thing.

The only change that I can see between your earlier and later writing is that it's no longer satirical. Your long essays are full of humor, but it's a kindly humor. Does that mean that you no longer have the satirical impulse?

Oh, I think the satirical stuff is a young man's business, isn't it? At first it's pure fun. After a while, if you do it long enough, it becomes a drag. That's true of comedy on television shows too. I used to stay up to watch *Saturday Night Live*. Now I try to go to bed before it comes on.

I don't understand what that has to do with age.

The show has aged. And the *age* has aged. Writing of all sorts comes out of an age. It's like painting. You write a certain book at a certain time in your life. It may be that the time for satire has passed. When I started writing the "Observer" column in '62, there'd been ten years of Eisenhower and nobody had written anything amusing in the paper for years. So if you wrote something even slightly irreverent about the president, people would say, "Gosh, that's pretty fresh!"

Was it also risky?

Yeah, it was, because almost anything you said that was slightly irreverent was satire. You forget what a closed culture the Eisenhower era was. After Kennedy was elected, everything was open, sassy, fresh. But I think wit has pretty much died out.

In Growing Up *you wrote that there would be a dividing line between the people born and raised before World War II and those born after.*

I feel that now. Another generation has taken over. You're not of their world any more. The experience of growing up in the Depression and pre-war America makes you a very alien character. You have a sense of being displaced by time.

After a certain age, I think you begin to feel that most of the people around you are strangers. And not only do they talk and think differently, they look *different. The young women are so tall now that they seem to belong to a different race.*

They all have those artificial faces that you can get now—not even human. But, yes, it's interesting how much taller people are now.

Of course, you're pretty tall yourself.

Well, I was six-two at one time. I've come down a bit [*chuckles*]. Six-two used to be considered tall. Now it's anything but. Every once in a while—frequently, in fact—I'll see a kid who looks six-six and weighs 275 pounds. These are enormous kids!

Are they obese?

No, I'm not talking fat. I'm talking big. Big bones, tall, big all over. When I was at Antietam, the Civil War battlefield, I went inside the museum. They had a lot of uniforms of men who had fought there and they looked like children's clothes. I suddenly realized how small they were and how much bigger my generation was. There's a picture of Abraham Lincoln with his generals at Richmond right after the war, and the generals come up to his chest. He was six-two, six-three. I realized how big he must have looked to people in his own time. And now I see these kids and *I* feel small. There *is* a generational change.

In one of your "Observer" columns about growing old, "The Pundit Warms Up," you made fun of your, or your persona's, waning memory—not being able to remember what was in a book you had read three days before, and so on. That happens to all of us, but memory loss can be a serious occupational hazard for a writer, can't it?

Oh, yes. You swear you remember things were just that way, and then you check and find you're wrong.

Do names or words ever disappear when you need them?

I have a little of that now—*names* I have trouble with—but it's not alarming. What I find about age and writing is that I write much more slowly. When I wrote the column, it went like this [*Baker mimes typing with his hands flying over the keys*]. Someone would ask, "How long does it take you to write a column?" and I'd say four hours. I'd sit around for two-and-a-half or three hours deciding what I was going to write, and once I started, it would go without a pause on the typewriter. I can't do that anymore.

Could that be because of the kind of writing you're doing now—long critical essays? Or do you attribute it solely to age?

It's age, sure. Things don't work as fast as they used to, and that includes your brain. Writing a column was like swimming underwater. When you swim underwater and you want to swim across the pool, you do it in one breath, right? You take a breath and you dive in and swim. When you're out of breath, you're on the other side. The column was like that. It's one smooth motion and it's over. But writing one of these *New York Review* pieces—I'll spend days on them. I'll think about different approaches, ways of dividing the piece, themes that I want to develop, and so forth. Then when I start writing, the writing is stiff. It's harder. The brain is beginning to calcify.

Do you revise these pieces a lot? You didn't revise the columns, did you?

Oh, sure. I always revised the columns. After I'd written them, I'd go back and do a heavy revision. But I'd do it all very quickly at the desk and I didn't brood about it for days. You couldn't, with a column. It had to be turned in that afternoon. With these pieces, yeah, I'll go back and rewrite and churn something out.

Do you ever face the blank page or the blank screen and feel, Oh God, what will I say?

That was a problem with the column, more than with these pieces. "Jeez, if I can't think of anything today, they're going to fire me. The presses are warming up down there."

What about your energy?

[*Long, theatrical moan of pain*] Ooooooh! I wish you hadn't brought that up. I'm usually asleep at this time [*looks at watch*], three-thirty. But to accommodate you, I took a keep-awake pill.

You didn't!

Well, yeah, because, you know, your energy is just gone by this time of the day. And so I nap. I lie down for an hour, and when I wake up I feel O.K.

Do you get up early?

It depends. If you're writing, you've got to get up early. I find that after lunch, my energy's gone. When I did that rather long Mellon piece, I would get up at about six o'clock and have breakfast and then write until about noontime.

About five hours?

I never write for five hours.

You can't do that?

I can, but it won't be any good. I could write for *eight* hours, but you'd throw away everything from the last five hours. After three hours, it's getting tired and it would almost need to be redone.

I want to thank you very much for doing this and I'm grateful to you for foregoing your nap.

[*Laughs*] I've made some coffee. Do you like coffee?

Chapter Notes

The first reference to each work is listed in the Notes. Subsequent references to the same work are indicated by their page numbers in parentheses in each chapter. The publication date refers to the edition of the work that was consulted, not to the date of the work's initial publication.

Introduction

1. Ronald Blythe, Introduction, *The View in Winter: Reflections on Old Age* (New York: Harcourt Brace Jovanovich, 1979), 10.
2. Shakespeare, *Henry IV, Part I*, Act I, Scene 2, *Complete Works of Shakespeare* (New York: Oxford University Press, 1936).
3. Shakespeare, *Henry IV, Part II*, Act 5, Scene 5.
4. Jonathan Swift, *Gulliver's Travels*, Part III, Chapter X, Literature Project.
5. W. B. Yeats, "The Tower," in *The Tower: The Collected Poems of W. B. Yeats* (New York: Macmillan, 1956), 123.
6. John W. Rowe, M.D., and Robert O. Kahn, M.D., quoted in Jane Brody, "Good Habits Outweigh Genes as Key to a Healthy Old Age," *The New York Times*, April 21, 1996.
7. Ibid.
8. Gail Sheehy, quoted in Janet Maslin, "Those Wonder Years Don't Start Before 60," *The New York Times*, July 19, 1995.
9. Stanley Kunitz, "The Wild Braid," *Passing Through: The Later Poems, New and Selected* (New York: W.W. Norton, 1995), 111.
10. Russell Baker, "Intimations of Mortality," Sunday Observer, *The New York Times Magazine*, February 28, 1988.
11. Russell Baker, "Menace of the Random," Observer, *The New York Times*, July 25, 1981.

Chapter 1

1. New Historicism, a critical theory developed by Stephen Greenblatt, then a professor of English at the University of California, Berkeley, became influential in academic literary circles in the 1980s. Professor Greenblatt defined New Historicism

Chapter Notes

as "the relation between literature and history, the process through which certain remarkable works of art are at once embedded in a highly specific life-world and seem to pull free of that life-world," which sounded to me like academic-speak for what Pritchett had been doing all along (quoted in "Greenblatt Named University Professor of the Humanities," *Harvard University Gazette,* Sept. 21, 2000).

2. V. S. Pritchett, "The Early Dostoyevsky," *The Complete Essays* (London: Chatto & Windus, 1991), 815.
3. V. S. Pritchett, "Tea with Mrs. Bittell," *Collected Stories* (New York: Vintage, 1979), 483.
4. V. S. Pritchett, "A Spanish Balzac," *The Complete Essays* (London: Chatto & Windus, 1991), 881- 2.
5. V. S. Pritchett, *Midnight Oil* (New York: Modern Library Edition, 1994), 217. (Originally published in 1971 by Chatto & Windus, London.)
6. V. S. Pritchett, *A Cab at the Door* (New York: Modern Library Edition, 1994), 211. (Originally published in 1968 by Chatto & Windus, London.)
7. V. S. Pritchett, "As Old as the Century," in *The Turn of the Years* (New York: Random House, 1982), 32. (Originally published under the title "Looking Back at Eighty," *The New York Times Magazine*, December 14, 1980.)
8. V. S. Pritchett, "Growing Old," *The Complete Essays* (London: Chatto & Windus, 1991), 1107.
9. V. S. Pritchett, *Midnight Oil*, 391.
10. V. S. Pritchett, "Finite Variety," *The New York Review of Books*, Vol. 26, No. 17, November 8, 1979. All further citations are from the online version of this essay at www.nybooks.com.
11. V. S. Pritchett, "The Spree," *Collected Stories* (New York: Vintage, 1981), 395.
12. V. S. Pritchett, "On the Edge of the Cliff," *Collected Stories* (New York: Vintage, 1981), 459.
13. V. S. Pritchett, "The Image Trade," *A Careless Widow & Other Stories* (London: Chatto & Windus, 1989), 153.

Chapter 3

1. John Ciardi, "Poetry: Saturday Review's Quarterly Roundup," *Saturday Review*, Vol. XLI, No. 39, 1958, 18.
2. Stanley Kunitz, "Postscript," *The Poems of Stanley Kunitz 1928–1978* (Boston: Little, Brown, 1958), 210.
3. Stanley Kunitz, "After the Last Dynasty," *Passing Through: The Later Poems, New and Selected* (New York: W. W. Norton, 1995), 27.
4. Stanley Kunitz, "Indian Summer at Land's End," *Passing Through*, 58.
5. Stanley Kunitz, "Route Six," *Passing Through*, 105.
6. Stanley Kunitz, "Touch Me," *Passing Through*, 158.
7. Stanley Kunitz, "As Flowers Are," *The Poems of Stanley Kunitz 1928–1978* (Boston: Little, Brown, 1958), 102.
8. Stanley Kunitz, "For the Word Is Flesh," *The Poems of Stanley Kunitz 1928–1978* (Boston: Little, Brown, 1958), 190.

Chapter Notes

9. Stanley Kunitz, "The Portrait," *Passing Through*, 22.
10. Stanley Kunitz, "Quinnapoxet," *Passing Through*, 76.
11. Stanley Kunitz, "Three Floors," *Passing Through*, 52.
12. Stanley Kunitz, "Halley's Comet," *Passing Through*, 148.
13. Stanley Kunitz, "The Layers," *Passing Through*, 107.
14. Stanley Kunitz, "Passing Through," *Passing Through*, 130.
15. Stanley Kunitz, "The Long Boat," *Passing Through*, 132.
16. Stanley Kunitz, "From Feathers to Iron," *Next-to-Last Things: New Poems and Essays* (Boston: The Atlantic Monthly Press, 1985), 30–1.
17. Stanley Kunitz, "King of the River," Notes, *Passing Through*, 163.
18. Stanley Kunitz, "King of the River," *Passing Through*, 54.
19. Stanley Kunitz, "The Knot," *Passing Through*, 73.
20. Ibid., "The Snakes of September," *Passing Through*, 111–2.
21. Stanley Kunitz, "The Round," *Passing Through*, 128.

Chapter 5

1. Robert McCrum, in "Writing Is Something I Have to Do," *The Observer*, October 14, 2007.
2. Harold Bloom, quoted by Sarah Crown in "Doris Lessing Wins Nobel Prize," *The Guardian*, October 11, 2007.
3. Lesley Hazleton, "Doris Lessing on Feminism, Communism and 'Space Fiction,'" *The New York Times*, July 25, 1982.
4. Doris Lessing, Introduction, *The Golden Notebook* (New York: Simon & Schuster, 1973), ix.
5. Doris Lessing, *African Laughter: Four Visits to Zimbabwe* (New York: HarperCollins, 1992), 73.
6. Doris Lessing, *Under My Skin: Volume One of My Autobiography* (New York: HarperCollins, 1994), 371.
7. Doris Lessing, Preface, *The Diaries of Jane Somers* (New York: Vintage, 1984), i.
8. Doris Lessing, *The Diary of a Good Neighbor*, in *The Diaries of Jane Somers*, 13.
9. Doris Lessing, *Martha Quest* (London: M. Joseph, 1952), 102.
10. Doris Lessing, "An Old Woman and Her Cat," *Stories* (New York: Alfred A. Knopf, 1978), 429.
11. Doris Lessing, *If the Old Could...*, *The Diaries of Jane Somers* (New York: Vintage, 1984), 259.
12. Doris Lessing, *The Summer Before the Dark* (New York: Vintage, 1973), 35.
13. Ibid., 65.
14. Doris Lessing, *Love, Again* (New York: HarperCollins, 1995), 1.
15. Michiko Kakutani, "Who Exactly Is This Sexagenarian Sex Kitten?" *The New York Times*, March 15, 1996.
16. Diane Johnson, "Stiff Upper Lip," review of *The Lemon Table* by Julian Barnes, *The New York Review of Books*, October 21, 2004.
17. Doris Lessing, "Old," *Time Bites* (New York: HarperCollins, 2004), 215.

Chapter Notes

Chapter 7

1. Hermione Lee, "Lost in Transit," review of *Selected Stories of Mavis Gallant*, in *The Guardian*, March 6, 2004. Note: The book was published in the United States as *The Collected Stories of Mavis Gallant*.
2. Michael Ondaatje, Introduction, *Paris Stories by Mavis Gallant* (New York: New York Review Books, 2002), vii.
3. Russell Banks, Introduction, *Varieties of Exile by Mavis Gallant* (New York: New York Review Books, 2003), xii.
4. Francine Prose, *Harper's*, April 1, 2003.
5. John McGahern, "The Adult Mysteries," review of *Across the Bridge* by Mavis Gallant, *The New York Times*, September 12, 1993.
6. Jonathan Coe, review of *Selected Stories of Mavis Gallant*, London Review of Books, Vol. 10, No. 18, September 18, 1997.
7. Mavis Gallant, "Forain," *The Collected Stories of Mavis Gallant* (New York: Random House, 1996), 630.
8. Mavis Gallant, "A State of Affairs," *Collected Stories*, 642.
9. Mavis Gallant, Preface, *Collected Stories*, x.
10. Mavis Gallant, "Lena," *Collected Stories*, 821.
11. Mavis Gallant, "In Plain Sight," *Collected Stories*, 868.
12. Mavis Gallant, Preface, *Collected Stories*, xvi–xvii.

Chapter 9

1. Russell Baker, "A Few Words at the End," Observer, *The New York Times*, December 25, 1998.
2. Russell Baker, "A Summer Beyond Wish," Observer, *The New York Times*, July 4, 1978.
3. Russell Baker, "Saps of Now and Then," Observer, *The New York Times*, November 27, 1998.
4. Russell Baker, "No Place for Crybabies," Observer, *The New York Times*, May 29, 1998.
5. Russell Baker, "Fooling with Faces," Observer, *The New York Times*, December 4, 1990.
6. Russell Baker, "Don't Believe It, Kids," Observer, *The New York Times*, November 20, 1998.
7. Russell Baker, "Hunting That Fountain," Observer, *The New York Times*, April 3, 1998.
8. Russell Baker, "A Shudder of Disgust," Observer, *The New York Times*, August 7, 1998.
9. Russell Baker, "It Was a Very Good Year," Observer, *The New York Times*, March 10, 1999.
10. Russell Baker, "Wish You Were Here," Observer, *The New York Times*, December 9, 1997.
11. Russell Baker, Introduction, *Looking Back* (New York: New York Review Books, 2002), x.

Chapter Notes

12. Russell Baker, "Love Boat," *Looking Back*, 127.
13. Russell Baker, "Troublemaker," *The New York Review of Books*, Vol. 51, No. 13, August 12, 2004. All further citations refer to the online version of this essay at www.nybooks.com.
14. Russell Baker, *The Good Times* (New York: William Morrow, 1989), 344.
15. Russell Baker, "Out of Step with the World," *Looking Back*, 173.
16. Russell Baker, *The Good Times*, 344.

Index

About Town 165
Adjani, Isabelle 118
Adler, Renata 164, 165, 167
African Laughter 76, 95, 99
"After the Last Dynasty" 54
Altersstil ("old-age style" in late works of painters and sculptors) 10
Alzheimer's 102, 192; *see also* dementia
The Anatomy of Melancholy 49
Ancient Mariner 41
Antietam 186
Appomattox 168
"As Flowers Are" 56
As Old as the Century 23–26, 31
Atlantic Monthly Press 54
Atwood, Margaret 139
"August" 146
Auschwitz 135, 146
Austria 144
"Autumn Day" 144–145
Avedon, Richard 134

baby boomers, aging of 11–12, 16, 151–159
Baker, Russell 13, 16–17, 149–177, 178–188
Baltimore 151
Baltimore Sun 181
Banks, Russell 105, 136–137
Barnes, Julian 94
Barry, Dave 181
Barszczewska, Elzbieta 117, 119
"Baum, Gabriel" 135
Beauvoir, Simone de 26–29, 30, 31
Beckett, Samuel 11, 26–27
Bennington College 53
Berlin Wall 111
Bernstein, Carl 157
Bloom, Harold 74–75
Blythe, Ronald 9, 26, 29, 30, 31
Bombeck, Irma 181
The Bonfire of the Vanities 173–174
Book of Job 180
Brighton, England 32, 37
Buchwald, Art 181

Bush, George W. 168–173
Byrd, Sen. Robert 17, 162, 167–173, 184

A Cab at the Door 22
Callaghan, Morley 139
Camden Town (London) 24–25
Camus, Albert 26
Canopus in Argus: Archives 77, 96, 98
The Canterbury Tales 10
Cape Cod 55, 65
A Careless Widow and Other Stories 42
The Castle 139
Chaucer, Geoffrey 10
Chekhov, Anton 138, 146
Christian Science Monitor 20
Ciardi, John 53
Civil War (Spain) 138
Civil War (United States) 178
Coe, Jonathan 106
Colette 148
the coming of age 9
The Coming of Age 26
concentration camp 111
"The Concert Party" 142
Council flat 15, 79, 82, 83
Council-run "Home" 84
Coupole 115, 127, 147

Dachau 116
"The Decadent Decade" 152
The Decline and Fall of the Roman Empire 26
De Gaulle, General Charles 117, 150
De Kooning, Willem 65
dementia 11, 16, 23, 113–114, 116, 123; *see also* Alzheimer's
demographics, change in twentieth century 11
Depression 14, 53, 175, 179
The Diaries of Jane Somers 15, 81
The Diary of a Good Neighbor 15, 77–81, 97
The Diary of Jane Somers 76
Dickens, Charles 174

Index

"The Diver" 45
Le Dôme 134, 148
"Don't Believe It, Kids" 154–156, 169
Dostoyevsky, Fyodor 20
Dowd, Maureen 181

Edison, Thomas 160
"Édouard, Juliette, Magdalena" 107, 120
Eisenhower, Pres. Dwight 150, 185
Elysée Palace 150
England 80, 91, 138
English Canada 144
English-Canadians 107
euphemisms 11; *see also* "politically correct speech"

Falstaff 10–11
Fine Arts Work Center, Provincetown 67
"Finite Variety" 29–31
Fitzgerald, F. Scott 142, 159, 161, 173
"Fooling with Faces" 153–154
"For the Word Is Flesh" 57
"Forain" 107, 108–112, 147
Forain, Blaise 108
fountain of youth 158
The Four-Gated City 75
"Four Seasons" 143
France 22, 23, 25, 46, 90, 97, 101, 108, 111, 114, 120, 122, 125, 130, 138, 143, 146, 147
France, Anatole 142
French Canada 144
French-Canadians 107
"From Feathers to Iron" 61
"The Fruit Tree" 94

Gallant, Mavis 13, 16, 105–133, 134–148
Gawande, Atul 134
Gill, Brendan 164, 175
Glass, Philip 96, 99
The Golden Notebook 75–76, 81, 94
Goldwater, Barry 162
Gone 165
Gonne, Maud 73
The Good Times 161, 171, 177
Gottlieb, Robert 166–167
Governor General's Award 138
"The Grandmothers" 89
Greek tragedy 28, 82, 163, 166
Green Water, Green Sky 143, 144, 146
"Growing Old" 26–29
Growing Up 170, 179, 180, 185
Gulliver's Travels 11
Guston, Philip 65

"Halley's Comet" 59–60
Hampstead (London) 85
Hardy, Thomas 24
Harvard 52
Hazelton, Lesley 75
Hearst, William Randolph 149, 162
"Henri Grippes" 107, 125
Henry IV 10
Henry IV, Part II 10–11
Here at the New Yorker 164
"Home Truths" 107
"Hunting That Fountain" 156–158

"I Dreamed That I Was Old" 65
If the Old Could... 15, 81, 86–90
"The Image Trade" 42–44, 45, 48
images of age 10, 11, 12, 13, 154; *see also* myths of age; stereotypes of age
"In Plain Sight" 107, 125–133
"In the War" 142
"Indian Summer at Land's End" 54–55
Intellectual Things 54
"Intimations of Mortality" 16
Iran 44
Iraq 168
Ireland 20, 22, 72
"It Was a Very Good Year" 158–159

January-May marriage 9
Johnson, Lyndon 162, 170–172
Johnson, Samuel 19

Kafka, Franz 139
Kakutani, Michiko 94
Keats, John 25, 69
Kempton, Murray 16, 162
Kennedy, John F. 185
Kennedy, Robert F. 162
Kennedy, Ted 171
A Kind of Order, a Kind of Folly 72
King Lear (character) 41, 167
King Lear (play) 9
"King of the River" 15, 61–62
Kline, Franz 65
Ku Klux Klan 170, 172
Kunitz, Stanley 13, 14, 52–64, 65–73

"Lady Olga" 174
Lawrence, D.H. 66
"The Layers" 60, 72
Lee, Hermione 105, 106
Leesburg, Virginia 175
"Lena" 107, 120–125
Lessing, Doris 13, 15, 74–95, 96–104

Index

"Let It Pass" 142
life cycle 15, 60
life expectancy, increase in twentieth century 9, 11, 23, 30
Lincoln, Abraham 186
The Living Novel 19
London 16, 20, 22, 25, 26, 31, 33, 45, 77, 80, 90, 93, 181
"The Long Boat" 61
Looking Back 161
Losing America 167–169, 172, 184
loss of friends in old age 26
Love, Again 16, 89, 90–94
"The Love Boat" 162–167

"Madeleine's Birthday" 137
Manhattan 159; *see also* New York; New York City
Marching Spain 20
Masterpiece Theatre 183
Maxwell, William 140–141
May-December romance 38, 89, 94
McCrum, Robert 74
McGahern, John 105
Mehta, Vad 163, 165
Mencken, H.L. 181
"The Merchant's Tale" 10
Midnight Oil 11, 19, 21–23, 24, 28, 32, 43
Mitchell, Joseph 17, 162, 173–175, 184
Mitterand, François 130
Molloy, Malone Dies, and *The Unnamable* trilogy 11
Le Monde 112
Montparnasse (Paris) 109, 115, 126, 133, 134
Montreal, Quebec 107
Montreal *Standard* 134
Montreal Stories 137
Morristown, Virginia 151
Motherwell, Robert 65
Munroe, Alice 105
"My Heart Is Broken" 142
myths of age 11, 13; *see also* images of age; stereotypes of age

Nansen passports 116
National Book Award 52
the "new old age" 12, 13
New Passages: Mapping Your Life Across Time (Gail Sheehy) 12
New Statesman 20
New York 55, 64, 135, 145, 159–160, 165, 167, 173–175, 177; *see also* Manhattan; New York City

New York City 52, 96, 52, 178; *see also* Manhattan; New York
New York Herald Tribune 175, 184
New York Journal American 149
New York Review of Books 17, 136, 161, 183, 187
New York Times 12, 16–17, 94, 148, 149, 161–162
The New Yorker 105, 134, 140, 148, 163–167, 184
Newhouse, S.I. 166
Nixon, Richard 162
"No Place for Crybabies" 152–153
Nobel Prize 74, 110
nursing homes 16, 23, 28, 121

"Observer" 16, 149, 150, 151, 162, 168
Oedipus at Colonus 9
"Old" 95–97
old age in literature 9
"An Old Woman and Her Cat" 81–86, 97
"On the Edge of the Cliff" 14, 38–42
Ondaatje, Michael 105, 136
Ondine 118
Ortega y Gasset 70
osteoporosis 141, 148
"Out of Step with the World" 173–177

Paris 16, 20–22, 107–109, 111–116, 118, 121–122, 124, 126, 134, 148
Paris Stories 136, 146
"Passing Through" 60
Passing Through: The Later Poems, New and Selected 52, 60
"The Pegnitz Junction" 106, 139–140, 142
Pérez Galdós, Benito 20–21
"Peter Pan" 158
Poets House 67
Polish émigrés 107, 108, 109, 113, 147
politically correct speech 154–156; *see also* euphemisms
Pompidou, Pres. Georges 118
"The Portrait" 57–58
"Postscript" 54
Pritchett, Dorothy 22, 45
Pritchett, V.S. 13, 14, 19–44, 45–51, 105
Prose, Francine 105
Proust, Marcel 159
Provincetown, Mass. 55, 65, 67
Pulitzer Prize 53, 180
"The Pundit Warms Up" 186

Quebec 142
Queen Elizabeth 181

Index

Queens (New York) 139; *see also* New York; New York City
"Quinnapoxet" 58

"Raccoon Journal" 73
Rayburn, Sam 169
Regent's Park (London) 25, 46
Remembering Mr. Shawn's New Yorker 163–164
retirement, compulsory 27, 30, 32, 33, 102
Richardson, Samuel 47
Richler, Mordecai 139
Roethke, Theodore 53
Ross, Harold 163, 166
Ross, Lillian 164, 165
Rothko, Mark 65
"The Round" 62–64
"Route Six" 55–56

"Saps of Today and Yesterday" 152
Saturday Night Live 185
Schubert, Franz 115, 119
sclerosis 145
"Secrets of the Flesh" 148
"Seinfeld" 156–158
Selected Poems of Stanley Kunitz, 1928–1958 53
"self-help" books on aging 12–13
"self of old age" 48
The Senate of the Roman Republic 171
sexuality in old age 14–16, 28, 30–31, 41, 73, 92
Shakespeare, William 9, 10, 25, 176
Shawn, William 17, 162–167
Sheehy, Gail 12, 13
Silvers, Robert 161, 184
"The Snakes of September" 15, 62, 64
Sophocles 9–10
South of France 90, 91, 143
Southern Rhodesia 13, 76; *see also* Zimbabwe
space fiction 75, 96
Spain 20, 22, 134
"The Spree" 14, 31–38
"A State of Affairs" 107, 112–119, 148
Stendhal 90
stereotypes of age 10; *see also* images of age; myths of age
Successful Aging 12
"successful aging" 12–13, 16
The Summer Before the Dark 87, 89
"A Summer Beyond Wish" 151
Sunday Observer 182

Swedish Academy 74
Swift, Jonathan 11, 156

"Tea with Mrs. Bittell" 20
The Testing-Tree 53, 57
Thomas, Lewis 9, 13
"Three Floors" 58–59
Thurber, James 163–164
"Touch Me" 15, 56
The Tower 11
"Troublemaker" 167–173
Truman, Harry 173
Twain, Mark 150, 181

Under My Skin 76
United States 27, 138, 149
U.S. House of Representatives 169
U.S. Senate 168, 170, 172
University of Toronto 144
"An Unmarried Man's Summer" 143
Unterberg Poetry Center 52
Up in the Old Hotel 178

Varieties of Exile 136
"Varieties of Exile" 137
Vienna 146
Vietnam 169, 171
The View in Winter 9, 26, 29

Warner, Sylvia Townsend 141
Watergate 157
Welsh coast 39
Welty, Eudora 105
Wharton, Edith 173
White House 168–169, 172
The Wild Braid 64
Wilde, Oscar 143
"Wish You Were Here" 159–161
Wolfe, Tom 173–174
Women's Liberation 76
Woodward, Bob 157
Worcester, Mass. 58, 59
Wordsworth 14, 73, 106
World War I 14, 25, 46, 101
World War II 14, 16, 20, 82, 108–116, 126, 134, 175, 185

Yagoda, Ben 165, 167
The Years with Ross 163
Yeats, W.B. 11, 72–73
YouTube 74

zeitgeist 75
Zimbabwe 13, 76

www.ingramcontent.com/pod-product-compliance
Lightning Source LLC
Chambersburg PA
CBHW032102300426
44116CB00007B/854